Family Home Evening for Me

A RESOURCE MANUAL

Family Home Evening for Me

A RESOURCE MANUAL

by Tamara Leigh Woolley

Horizon
Springville, Utah

ISBN 13: 978-0-88290-935-6
ISBN 10: 0-88290-935-5

Published by Horizon, an imprint of Cedar Fort, Inc., 2373 W. 700 S.,
Springville, Utah 84663
Distributed by Cedar Fort, Inc., www.cedarfort.com

LIBRARY OF CONGRESS CATALOGING-IN-PUBLICATION DATA

Woolley, Tamara Leigh.
Family home evening for me : a resource manual / by Tamara Leigh Woolley.
p. cm.
Includes bibliographical references.
ISBN 0-88290-935-5
1. Family--Religious life. 2. Church of Jesus Christ of Latter-day Saints--Doctrines. 3. Mormon Church--Doctrines. I. Title.

BX8643.F3W66 2006
248.4'89332--dc22

2006025595

Cover designed by Nicole Williams

Typeset by Natalie Roach

Printed in the United States of America

10 9 8 7 6 5 4 3 2 1

Printed on acid-free paper

For Tara Duffin, Dad, and the members of the Tokyo Third Ward

Contents

Introduction....1

Getting Started....3

Setting and Achieving Goals....7

Organization....13

FHE Record....14

Putting It All Together....21

Section 1: Spiritual Focus
An Idea for Every Week of the Year....23

Section 2: Social Focus
An Idea for Every Week of the Year....87

Section 3: Temporal Focus
An Idea for Every Week of the Year....141

List of Focus Topics....195

Sources....197

About the Author....199

Introduction

And the options are . . . *Family Home Evening with Small Children* and *Family Home Evening with Teenagers!*

Not much help for a thirty-year-old single member of the Church trying to have her own Family Home Evenings. What about books and manuals specific to my needs? Nothing. *Ensign* articles? One written by a faithful widow in the July 1997 *Ensign*. So is it really important that I even try? Yes.

President James E. Faust said, "Whether we are young or old, single or married, whether we have children at home or have become empty nesters, family home evening can increase unity and love in our homes. Family home evening is for everyone (James E. Faust, "Enriching Our Lives through Family Home Evening," *Ensign*, June 2003, 3).

No matter what your circumstances are, you are always included in the family unit consisting of a loving Heavenly Father and an elder brother Jesus Christ. Where there is a family unit, there is an opportunity to enjoy the blessings that come from family home evening. I wanted these blessings, but my efforts at conducting family home evening were sporadic, without direction, and ultimately boring. Something had to be done. I wanted to participate in this important program of the Church as a single member and realized that if this was the case with me, then there must be others with this same desire. Also, in my quest to do right, if I was feeling a lack of assistance and resources, surely I wasn't the only one with these obstacles. Taking a positive and active approach to the problem, I decided not to complain about my situation but rather to find a solution to my frustrations. The result was this book. There is strength in the Lord's words: "But he that doeth the will of God abideth forever" (1 John 2:17).

Wonderful blessings have come into my life as I have put into practice what is written on these pages. I am not just conditioning a habit, but forming an eternal part of my character as I strive to follow the path that God has laid out before me. My prayer is that the suggestions in this book may be a starting place and an inspiration for all of you who need some help with family home evening but don't know where to find it. Good luck!

Getting Started

A Willing and Positive Attitude

You have heard it over and over again: "It is often difficult to change circumstances, but a positive attitude can help lift discouragement" (Val R. Christensen, "Overcoming Discouragement," *Ensign*, November 1998, 31). Family home evening is no exception. A positive attitude is essential for success in catching and maintaining the exciting spirit of family home evening. Holding regular family home evenings in your home with just yourself, the Holy Ghost, and your goldfish is no easy task. However, some of your hesitant and sceptical feelings may be quelled if you evaluate the reasons for your decision to make this important step in your life.

Somewhere along the way, you picked up this book because you heeded a prompting from the Holy Ghost. Through this prompting, you realized that you needed to improve your current standard of family home evening commitment or begin participating in this vital church program. In so doing, one accepts the guidance of a loving Heavenly Father, and so the power of heaven is unleashed to help you obey; "and my Spirit shall be in your hearts, and mine angels round about you, to bear you up" (D&C 84:88).

Obedience, Courage, and Enthusiasm

Whatever your preconceived thoughts about family home evening, your willingness to at least set foot on this righteous path shows an attitude of obedience and courage. These are crucial character traits to possess in order to be successful in your family home evening endeavors.

Now, take these attitudes of obedience and courage and combine them with enthusiasm. Enthusiasm not only for the first week or first month of family home evening but a lifelong enthusiasm for growth in the gospel of Jesus Christ through this program. Your life will be blessed. So will many lives of the people around you as they see your increased testimony and love for the basic teachings of the Church.

Discouragement

While cultivating enthusiasm, there is one negative attitude that may creep in and slow your progress. Discouragement can quickly tear down your commitment to improve your testimony of family home evening. If things don't seem to be working the way you planned, then make a change. Finding a time, place, day (if Monday nights are inconvenient), and changing the length of your activities or your expectations can help you to balance out the opposition from Satan. He does not want you to prosper. If you keep a record of each week's family home evening and any positive experiences that occur, it can help you recall and recognize the progress you are making. You must not go to sleep until you have found at least one positive outcome from each family home evening, such as:

- I planned and carried out family home evening without distraction.
- I increased my testimony in an area of the gospel.
- I blessed the lives of others through service.

- I strengthened my relationships with others as we participated together.
- I developed a new skill.
- I achieved my purpose during my family home evening.

Enthusiasm can only be maintained, and discouragement overcome, if you see success and blessings coming from your efforts. The challenge is to feel as Alma did when he said, "the Lord doth give me exceedingly great joy in the fruit of my labors" (Alma 36:25), no matter how small those fruits may seem.

Priorities

Family home evening is high on your priority list if you feel it necessary to make a more conscious effort in this area. But is it the highest? Is your desire to follow the prophets' counsel concerning family home evening more important than any temporal distractions? It is easy to say, "No, thank you," to invitations on Sunday because you know it is the Sabbath day. Is it also that easy to say the same if events clash with your scheduled family home evening time? Your family home evening schedule should be flexible, and some activities will need to be held at different times or days. But these activities could still be incorporated as the focus of your family home evenings. Just keep in mind that the trap of using any excuse to postpone your weekly family home evenings will quickly become common practice. Eventually, family home evening will be right back where it started—a thought in the back of your mind.

For most, family home evening is not a new or foreign concept. There are those of you who have already committed a major part of your lives to diligently holding family home evenings with your own children but are now living apart from them. Now is not the time to rest, "for blessed is he that endureth to the end" (Alma 38:2). You are at a greater advantage than those (myself included) who have not yet had the sacred opportunity to raise children or who did not participate in family home evening during their own childhood. Call upon your experiences and adapt the program you know so well to suit your circumstances now. You don't have to start from scratch.

Be happy. Recognize and periodically review definite benefits coming from family home evening. This will maintain a willingness to continue in the tradition you have forged for your own growth and that of your posterity. Enthusiasm, obedience, and looking for the positives are solid blocks with which to build a foundation for your family home evenings. Once these are stable, family home evening can then begin to have personal meaning as you ask yourself and respond to the question: "What do I want to achieve?"

Setting and Achieving Goals

What do you want to see as a result of your participation in the family home evening program? During the majority of your family home evenings, only you and the Spirit of the Lord will be in attendance. Take this time to refine areas of your life that need a little polishing or even a good spring cleaning. Three main areas of goal setting can encompass the purposes President Joseph F. Smith envisioned when he instituted this program. These are as follows: First, hold regular family home evening and increase your testimony of its importance in your life as an individual child of God; second, have family home evening aid you in progressing spiritually, socially, and temporally; and third, have fun!

Hold Regular Family Home Evenings

As with any goal, setting it is easy; accomplishing your goals requires effort. All that we do during our mortal probation should be geared toward gaining and increasing our testimonies of righteous principles that will lead us back to our Father in heaven. Family home evening, as one of those principles, is no different. President Gordon B. Hinckley has stated:

> The more often you go [to the temple], the more certainly you will know of the truth of this great work in the house of the Lord. If you worry in your minds about the law of tithing, pay your tithing. And with the payment of your tithing will

> come a conviction of the truth of that law as the Lord's law of finance, and so it is with every principle of the gospel of Jesus Christ: the Word of Wisdom, the welfare program, the family home evening program. Every principle which God has revealed carries its own conviction of truth. (Gordon B. Hinckley, "News of the Church," *Ensign*, April 1996, 74)

The way to gain this "conviction of truth" is to live the principle and recognize the associated blessings. We will discuss the practical side of accomplishing your goal—to continually have family home evening every week—later, but the desire must ultimately come from the seeds planted in your heart. Commit to succeed, and then pray. Heavenly Father knows you—your name, your circumstances, your dreams, your hopes, and most of all, he knows your potential.

But who, in their busy life, has time to take an evening off each week? Who has time to spend precious hours on extra church activities when they already hold numerous callings? Who can afford to delay tasks over spending time on herself? Who has time to do everything that is asked of him? Those who recognize the love of Jesus Christ through the companionship of the Holy Ghost have time. Those who labor diligently and faithfully to keep the sacred covenants that they have made with God have time. Those who know where their eternal rewards can be found have time. You have time. "*With men this is impossible; but with God all things are possible*" (Matthew 19:26; emphasis added).

Developing Spiritually, Socially, and Temporally Through Family Home Evening

Setting goals in family home evening to progress in three different areas of your life can help you to maintain balance and enrich already established efforts to focus on those things that are "virtuous, lovely, or of good report or praiseworthy" (Articles of Faith 1:13). I chose the three areas of spiritual, social, and temporal well being on which to focus my family home evening suggestions. The concepts printed on these pages are neither new nor profound. However, through these three specific areas, a wide variety of opportunities present themselves for you to discover the blessings of family home evening and the positive role it plays in coming to know our Savior and ourselves. Choosing family home evening focuses from areas that are relevant to you at a particular time will assist you in moving forward. Some ideas may not fit neatly into one particular category, or you may just be in need of a fun, relaxing night. Do not be concerned if you cannot place your family home evening focus into a defined slot. It is the performance and outcome of the activity that is important.

I do not hold such great faith in my ability to give suggestions; but rather, I have faith that those who are earnestly searching for help to become a better son or daughter of God will receive the aid they require. That help will ultimately come from a concerned and involved source, "for your Father, who is in Heaven, knoweth that you have need of all these things" (D&C 84:83). Family home evening is one time where your pleas for guidance and strength can, by the power of God, answer your prayers and better your life.

Have Fun

Even when one has the best of intentions, the most focussed goal setting, and a burning testimony of the will of God, disheartenment will occur if family home evening nights are *boring*! This is a program of the gospel that was designed to bring joy into living the teachings of Jesus Christ, as David B. Haight explains:

> All over the world Monday evening has been set aside by the First Presidency as family night.

> A night of participation, involvement, and wholesome fun. . . . Every home in the Church has been instructed to build a solid foundation for sound citizenship and active church participation. (David B. Haight, "A Foundation Whereon Men Cannot Fall," *Ensign*, July 1972, 107)

"Every home" includes your home. "Wholesome fun" includes pleasure within the bounds that the Lord has set and striving to enjoy all that is around you, despite uncontrollable circumstances. Remember, you can have as much fun discovering how to feel the Spirit of God as you can spending time on temporal recreations.

You are able to apply the wonderful gift of agency through family home evening. You get to choose what you do each week. You know what needs to be done. You can make it happen. With wisdom from the Holy Ghost, you can plan and participate in family home evenings that will place a smile on your face, leave satisfaction in your heart, and brighten the glow of your spirit. I believe we should be optimistic and convince our associates that truth, honor, virtue, and every other type of righteousness will win. I believe with President Joseph F. Smith that:

> Leaders of the Church . . . should be men [and women] not easily discouraged, not without hope, and not given to forebodings of all sorts of evils to come. Above all things the leaders of the people should never disseminate a spirit of gloom in the hearts of the people. If men standing in high places sometimes feel the weight and anxiety of momentous times, they should be all the firmer and all the more resolute in those convictions which come from a God-fearing conscience and pure lives. Men in their private lives should feel the necessity of extending encouragement

> to the people by their own hopeful and cheerful intercourse with them, as they do by their utterances in public places. It is a matter of the greatest importance that the people be educated to appreciate and cultivate the bright side of life rather than permit its darkness and shadows to hover over them (*Gospel Doctrine*, 155). Personally, I am convinced that those who keep the commandments God has given and those which he will yet give in these latter days are in a position to be and will be as the righteous ten who, could they have been found, would have been in the days of Sodom and Gomorrah. ("News of the Church," *Ensign*, September 1973, 83)

The leaders President Smith refers to are you. You are a leader in your community, ward, stake, circles of friends and acquaintances, and in any situation in which you find yourself. The happiness and delight with which you can hold family home evenings will rub off and touch all that you do from day to day, week to week, and into eternity.

Once you have set personal goals for your family home evening, confirmation by the power of the Holy Ghost that this is the desire of God for you at this time will be a great support in helping you to achieve them. Some goals may take years to achieve, while others can be accomplished in a single night. Whatever the time frame, remember not to be too hard on yourself. Perfection comes "line upon line, precept upon precept, here a little and there a little" (2 Nephi 28:30), and family home evening is no exception. Sometimes we need to be reminded:

> Surely the Lord God will bless and honor those who meet their obligations and sacrifice their time, talents, and means in helping build the

> kingdom of God on this earth. By latter-day revelation the Lord promises those who are faithful, "For thus saith the Lord—I, the Lord, am merciful and gracious unto those who fear me, and delight to honor those who serve me in righteousness and in truth unto the end. Great shall be their reward and eternal shall be their glory" (D&C 76:5–6). (Adney Y. Komatsu, "The Blessing of Building a Temple," *Ensign*, May 1976, 101)

These promises are real and worth every step you take toward them. Decide to start today to do all that you can to make them available in your life.

Organization

For some, this will be the hardest part of the successful family home evening process. For others, it will be the easiest. Whichever side of the coin your talent for organization lies, organization will be needed. You need to start by preparing to be organized. Once mental and spiritual preparation are obtained, through our previously discussed areas of maintaining a positive attitude and goal setting, we move into the hands-on portion of family home evening. Being a super-organized person myself, I find it helpful to have lists, charts, and calendars strung around my home to help me keep track of all that I need to do. This has spilled over into my family home evenings. President Kimball's words, "From time immemorial the Lord has counselled us to be record-keeping people" (Spencer W. Kimball, "President Kimball Speaks Out on Personal Journals," *Ensign,* December 1980, 61), are not only true for Church membership records, journals, and family histories but in all that we do in which the record has the potential to influence future generations for good. The next page has a copy of what I have simply called the FHE Record.

FHE RECORD

DATE: ____

VENUE: ____

OPENING HYMN: ____________________________________

OPENING PRAYER: __________________________________

SCHEDULE REVIEW: _________________________________

____

FOCUS: ____

____

____

____

CLOSING HYMN: ____________________________________

CLOSING PRAYER: __________________________________

TREAT: ____

POSITIVE OUTCOMES: _______________________________

____

____

NEXT WEEK/PREPARATION: ___________________________

____

____

____

It is not the most spectacular plan you will ever find, but its purpose is more important than its presentation.

Date and Venue

These are standard for any record so that your posterity can recall the when and where of spiritual and temporal experiences. It will also be encouraging to see the consistency with which you are participating in family home evening.

Opening and Closing Hymns and Prayers

Family home evening is a program of The Church of Jesus Christ of Latter-day Saints, and as such should be conducted with opening and closing hymns and prayers as we read in the Bible: "Let the word of Christ dwell in you richly in all wisdom; teaching and admonishing one another in psalms and hymns and spiritual songs, singing with grace in your hearts to the Lord" (Colossians 3:16).

Feel free to sing the only hymn in your repertoire over and over if that is all your talent allows. Remember that there are CDs to sing along to, musical instruments to play, or perhaps just the hymn book to open. One great thing about being by yourself for the majority of your family home evening nights is that whatever your skill in carrying a tune, you are the only one who will hear it! What Heavenly Father will hear is the sincerity with which you sing praises unto him and his beloved Son. Selecting hymns that have relevance to your focus for the evening can heighten the spiritual experiences that are available. The First Presidency has counseled us to use the hymns to invite the Spirit into our lives:

> Brothers and sisters, let us use the hymns to invite the Spirit of the Lord into our congregations, our homes, and our personal lives. Let us memorize and ponder them, recite and sing them,

> partake of their spiritual nourishment. Know that the song of the righteous is a prayer unto our Father in Heaven, "and it shall be answered with a blessing upon [your] heads." (First Presidency Preface, *Hymns* [1985], x)

The singing of sacred hymns invites the Spirit and shows gratitude toward our Savior. Prayer takes this worship a step further, for "ye must not perform any thing unto the Lord save in the first place ye shall pray unto the Father in the name of Christ, that he will consecrate thy performance unto thee, that thy performance may be for the welfare of thy soul" (2 Nephi 32:9). By opening and closing family home evening in the name of Jesus Christ, our labors are sanctified. We have the chance to use that hallowed time to advance our lives under the direction of the Godhead—their purpose being our perfection. We have been promised that "when we honor our Heavenly Father in our homes, He will honor our efforts" (Neil L. Andersen, "Prophets and Spiritual Mole Crickets," *Ensign*, November 1999, 17).

Schedule Review

This may not be a necessary or regular part of your family home evening, especially if held on a day other than Sunday or Monday. It is, however, a quiet opportunity to sit and counsel with yourself about matters and concerns that have arisen in the past or that may occur during the next week. A brief outline of what you should have accomplished and what you need to accomplish can help you keep things in perspective. Through this brief assessment of your life each week, you are able to evaluate your obedience to the commandment given by the Lord:

> Verily I say, men should be anxiously engaged in a good cause, and do many things of their own free will, and bring to pass much righteousness;

> for the power is in them, wherein they are agents unto themselves. And inasmuch as men do good they shall in no wise lose their reward. (D&C 58:27–28)

Focus

Here we come to the nitty-gritty of your family home evening program. By selecting an area of focus and a task that will enable you to improve in that area, family home evening is born! The scope of your focus is unlimited. Your interests, resources, time, finances, and testimony will all determine what you choose to concentrate on from one week to the next. Included in this book are ideas that you may wish to use, adapt to your own circumstances and needs, or dismiss altogether. Whatever your decision, you must have a focus for each family home evening for it to be successful.

"It is a false haven of rest for those who are content to live without purpose, commitment, or self-discipline," said Elder Marvin J. Ashton. "We must heed the words in Alma: 'Behold, this life is the time for men to prepare to meet God; yea, behold the day of this life is the day for men to perform their labors' (Alma 34:32)" (Marvin J. Ashton, "Straightway," *Ensign*, May 1983, 32).

Without a personal focus, it is impossible for the time spent during family home evening to help you do as Alma counseled above. Choose what has meaning for you. Focus on what will help you the most. Do what you know needs to be done.

Treat

Whether you are young or old, no family home evening is complete without a treat. Just as the scope of your focus is boundless, your treat options are just as flexible. Although it is a major source of enjoyment for most, you are not confined to food. Other alternatives can be found, but no matter your choice of treat, it must be in keeping with the spirit of family home evening. For example, choosing to watch a movie that does not meet the standards of the Church after an uplifting night of personal development will quickly diminish all that was accomplished. However, taking a relaxing bath and pondering the past couple of hours spent in the service of yourself, God, and your brothers and sisters, will enhance your experiences and keep your testimony burning long after you have said, "Amen."

Positive Outcomes

Wanting to achieve desired outcomes determines the choice of your focus before you begin your family home evening. As discussed briefly in *A Willing and Positive Attitude*, recognizing that these outcomes were achieved, and discovering further positive results is an element of your family home evening that comes after the fact, rather than before or during your experience. As suggested, do not put down your record until you have found at least one good thing that came as a consequence of the night's effort. Some weeks this will be easy and the results plentiful, while other weeks you may struggle to come up with anything except that you were obedient in following divine counsel to hold family home evening. This may seem like a meaningless addition to record keeping, but for those not prone to writing in a journal, it may be the only account of a testimony gained, feelings felt as service was given, goals achieved, or numerous other consequences that will become evident.

"We can make each home a house of faith by believing in the goodness of God and believing that we can live gospel principles and live in peace and security," said Elder Joseph B. Wirthlin. "We need to have the faith to be obedient, to keep trying, and to keep a positive outlook. Sometimes we get discouraged and feel like giving up. But as an old cowboy once said, 'If I get bucked off, I must get back up on the horse and ride on.' We can never give up (Joseph B. Wirthlin, "Spiritually Strong Homes and Families," *Ensign*, May 1993, 69).

How true these remarks are and how relevant they are to family home evening.

Next Week's Focus and Treat

To help you achieve a stress-free family home evening the following week, write a note to yourself about the focus and the treat. Another advantage is that over a period of time you can see in which direction you are taking your family home evening. You may find that you need to incorporate more than one focus area to keep balance or realize that concentrating on one theme for a time has helped you progress in a certain area. Whatever your experience, this will help you to discover what course of family home evening is the best for your eternal and temporal needs.

Preparation

This is a helpful tool in keeping family home evening a manageable part of your week. Briefly commenting on what you will need to organize for the following week after choosing a focus will naturally aid you in preparing for that event. If necessary, transfer these notes to your fridge, planner, or somewhere else where you will frequently see them, to serve as a constant reminder of the preparations that you need to make.

Although physical preparation is important, do not neglect the significance of spiritual preparation. Remember that we have been commanded to "organize [ourselves]; prepare every needful thing; and establish a house, even a house of prayer, a house of fasting, a house of faith, a house of learning, a house of glory, a house of order, a house of God" (D&C 88:119). This "house" as referred to in the Doctrine and Covenants can, and should be, your house. If you "prepare every needful thing," then your home will be filled with prayer, fasting, faith, learning, glory, order, and the love of God—not only on family home evening night but continually throughout every day of your life.

Putting It All Together

With the three instruments of a good attitude, clear goals, and firmly established organization, it is time to put them into practice. You are armed with all that is necessary for success in creating family home evenings that have power to bring further light from Christ into your life. Just be mindful of one trick the adversary may use to stall your efforts—procrastination.

Elder Henry B. Eyring said the following:

> All of us have faced deadlines. Fear can grip us when we realize that there may not be enough time left to finish what we promised we would do. The thought comes, "Why didn't I start earlier?" The Lord knew we would be tempted to procrastinate the most important preparation we would ever make in this life. More than once He warned us about delay. He taught the parable of the ten virgins, five of whom did not fill their lamps for the coming of the bridegroom. He also gave the parable of the servants who were faithless because they believed their Lord would delay His coming. The results of delay were tragic. (Henry B. Eyring, "Do Not Delay," *Ensign*, November 1999, 33)

The postponement of experiencing family home evening is not the most grievous of sins. However, not following through on a prompting by the Holy Ghost to incorporate it into your life, as with all promptings, may be detrimental to you reaching your potential within the period the Lord knows you are able. Do not let procrastination be a hindrance to your progression.

Elder Marvin J. Ashton counseled:

> Do not doubt your abilities. Do not delay worthy impressions. With God's help, you cannot fail. He will give you the courage to participate in meaningful change and purposeful living. . . . Those who fear, procrastinate. Those who change for the better show progress straightway and become wiser and stronger. We need to develop the courage to straightway take the first step. We need to remember that children learn to walk only because someone encourages them to take the first step. May we launch straightway toward setting goals that are gospel oriented, knowing that if we use the talents that are ours—that if we help others, strive for peace, avoid being overly sensitive or overly critical, strength upon strength will be added to our own abilities and we will move straightway toward greater growth, happiness, and eternal joys. Our Master and Savior invites us to straightway embrace His truths and enjoy the warmth of His constant companionship. (Marvin J. Ashton, "Straightway," *Ensign*, May 1983, 32)

Don't put off your promised blessings any longer—get to it!

Except a man be born of water and of the Spirit, he cannot enter into the kingdom of God.

—John 3:5

Section 1: Spiritual Focus

AN IDEA FOR EVERY WEEK OF THE YEAR

He shall hold the keys of the patriarchal blessing upon the heads of all my people, that whosoever he blesses shall be blessed.
—Doctrine and Covenants 124:92–93

1. JUST FOR YOU

Read and ponder the inspired words of your patriarchal blessing.

PURPOSE

To increase your testimony of your divine role in the Plan of Salvation.

PREPARATION

For those who have not yet received their Patriarchal Blessing, this is the evening to decide whether it is something you should pursue at this time. Have scriptures and *Ensign* articles ready to read on the subject. Be prepared to have the Holy Ghost influence your mind and heart as you make this important decision. Make concrete plans to call your bishop during the following week to schedule an interview if you feel that this is the desire of your Father in heaven.

If you possess a patriarchal blessing, find it! Make a photocopy of your blessing so that you can write notes and mark important passages on it that are relevant to you now. Have paper, pens, and marking pencils on hand. You can establish categories to outline your blessing, such as talents, warnings, promises, and consequences. As you read through your blessing, write down your impressions, mark passages, and open your heart to the expression of love that your Father in Heaven shows you through your blessing. Periodically review your patriarchal blessing and the notes you have written while pondering its meaning. Add to them as more inspiration comes.

POTENTIAL POSITIVE OUTCOMES

- Knowledge of where you came from, who you are, and your potential.
- A clear path of how to reach your potential
- Something that you can turn to for peace and comfort when you question your identity or worth as a child of God.

And that same God hath called me by a holy calling, to preach the word unto this people, and hath given me much success, in the which my joy is full. —Alma 29:13

2. MISSION IN LIFE

Read through your own, or someone else's mission journal.

PURPOSE

To rekindle your desire to proclaim the gospel.

PREPARATION

For those who have served full-time missions, find your mission journals. For those who have not, contact a member of your family or ward with whom you have a close relationship and ask to borrow his mission journals. Spend your family home evening reading through the honest, uncut, real-life experiences of missionaries.

POTENTIAL POSITIVE OUTCOMES

- Recollection of great happenings in your own life or the lives of your family and friends.
- An increased desire to make missionary work a part of your everyday life.
- An opportunity to learn from difficult times.
- Development of your testimony of the role of the Savior in every person's life.

Will ye answer me a few questions which I shall ask you?
—Alma 11:21

3. Q & A

Discuss some life and gospel questions with someone you know and trust.

PURPOSE

To strengthen you testimony through the wisdom and guidance of another.

PREPARATION

If you are not already in the habit, start keeping a notebook of the questions and thoughts you have as you read your scriptures daily and participate in Church meetings. When the notebook contains a substantial amount of questions and comments, it's time for this family home evening. Choose a member of your ward with whom you have a respectful relationship, perhaps your home or visiting teacher, Gospel Doctrine teacher or ward mission leader and their families. Spend this evening discussing the questions you have. This family home evening should not be used to confess sins, participate in controversial discussions, or speak negatively about doctrines of the gospel in any form. The feelings you should have as you finish this evening should be ones of peace, enlightenment, humility, and a desire to improve upon the life you are now living.

POTENTIAL POSITIVE OUTCOMES

- An increase of faith and testimony.
- Nourishment of relationships as others lead and guide you.
- Direction to improve your life.

And it shall come to pass in the last days, that the mountain of the Lord's house shall be established in the top of the mountains, and shall be exalted above the hills; and all nations shall flow unto it.

—Isaiah 2:2

4. TEMPLE WORSHIP

Whether it be an endowment, sealing, initiatory, or baptismal session, give some temple service.

PURPOSE

To increase your testimony of your role in the salvation of brothers and sisters who are living in the Spirit World.

PREPARATION

For some this will be a five-minute car ride, for others months of planning, budgeting, and organization. The most vital part of your preparation is to see that you hold, and are worthy to hold, a current temple recommend. Make interview arrangements with your bishop if necessary. As temples across the globe are closed on Monday, perhaps this week your family home evening night will be rescheduled. Physical preparation is important to ensure a calm, unrushed entrance through the temple doors. Spiritual preparation enables you to gain knowledge from the heavens and feel a closeness to those for whom you are performing the ordinances. Make sure that you are dressed appropriately and that your frame of mind is set on the things of the Spirit.

POTENTIAL POSITIVE OUTCOMES

- Expansion of gospel knowledge.
- An increased testimony about temple work.

- Satisfaction from obeying the call to redeem the dead.
- Confidence to face the week ahead.
- Renewal of relationships with friends and family members or acquaintances who attend the temple.

I will sing, yea, I will sing praises unto the Lord.

—Psalm 27:6

5. SING, SING A SONG

Practice singing hymns from the LDS hymn book that are unfamiliar to you.

PURPOSE

To feel comfortable singing any hymn at any time.

PREPARATION

You will need a copy of *Hymns of The Church of Jesus Christ of Latter-day Saints*; musical accompaniment is helpful. You may play your own musical instrument if talent and availability allows. If not, borrow or buy cassette tapes or compact discs containing recordings of the hymns. Mark all of the hymns with which you are unfamiliar. If there are many, select just a few to work on each evening. By playing or listening to the music numerous times and then singing the melody, practice each hymn until you can confidently sing it.

POTENTIAL POSITIVE OUTCOMES

- Recognition of the Spirit that comes through singing songs of worship.
- An increased confidence and ability to participate when hymns are sung.
- Replacement of unwelcome thoughts with sacred, wholesome music.

Surely the Lord God will do nothing, but he revealeth his secret unto his servants the prophets.

—Amos 3:7

6. SCRIPTURE HEROES

Select a prophet from one of the four standard works. Read and mark each scripture relative to him.

PURPOSE

To become more familiar with the teachings of Christ through the lives of his chosen ministers.

PREPARATION

Preselect a prophet to study, using prayer to make this decision. Look up all scriptural references relating to your chosen prophet. Have paper, pens, and marking pencils to write down inspired thoughts. Mark influential passages, and make notes about interesting facts that become evident to you. Acquire a picture of your chosen prophet, if available, to place before you while studying. This will assist you in increasing your testimony of the reality of the man and the divinity of his words.

POTENTIAL POSITIVE OUTCOMES

- An increased testimony about the reality of prophets and their role in the plan of salvation.
- Familiarization of the scriptures.
- Expansion of scripture study methods.
- Answers to questions or prayers from the experiences of a prophet of God.

They without us should not be made perfect.

—Hebrews 11:40

7. FAMILY HISTORY? HELP!

Visit your local family history center.

PURPOSE

To increase your testimony of the role that family history plays in the plan of salvation.

PREPARATION

Find the location of and directions to your nearest family history center. Remember that this may not necessarily be a Church-run facility, as many libraries have genealogy sections. Have questions ready to ask and/or family information you need to find. Strive to forget any negative or preconceived ideas you have about family history work.

POTENTIAL POSITIVE OUTCOMES

- Continuation of service to save the souls of countless members of your family.
- Acquirement of information that was previously unknown to you.
- A desire to "do your part, however great or small, in strengthening and binding your families together by engaging in temple work and the family history that supports it" (Mary Ellen Smoot, "Family History: A Work of Love," *Ensign*, Mar. 1999, 15).

And he who receiveth all things with thankfulness shall be made glorious; and the things of this earth shall be added unto him, even an hundred fold, yea, more.

—Doctrine and Covenants 78:19

8. GRATITUDE

Spend the evening writing letters of gratitude.

PURPOSE

To cultivate your ability to develop a more thankful heart.

PREPARATION

Think of numerous people, not just one or two, to whom you genuinely wish to write to thank. These people may be an old school teacher who made a difference, a sacrament speaker whose message touched you, visiting or home teachers who have helped you, or the bus driver who is always friendly. Obtain the appropriate addresses you will need. Have stationery, pens, and postage stamps ready to use. In some cases, e-mails may be sent if appropriate and a computer is readily available.

POTENTIAL POSITIVE OUTCOMES

- Appreciation for the profound impact that other people play in our lives.
- Incorporation of this aspect of the gospel deeper into your life.

Feast upon the words of Christ.

—2 Nephi 32:3

9. LISTEN

Listen to an inspirational talk.

PURPOSE

To become motivated by the experiences of others to live the gospel of Christ.

PREPARATION

Choose a cassette tape, compact disc, or a talk available on the Internet that contains messages of encouragement and examples of the influence of the gospel in the lives of members of the Church. If you do not own any tapes or CDs or if you are after something new, your ward library, friends, Church book stores, or your public library and the Internet are good resources. Some of your options are previous General Conference talks, recordings of firesides, tapes with a specific theme produced by the Church, or other sources known to be in harmony with gospel teachings. Remember that a quiet, peaceful time is essential for this evening.

POTENTIAL POSITIVE OUTCOMES

- An increased testimony of how aspects of the gospel can enrich your life.
- Influential promptings from the Holy Ghost to help you improve your commitment to follow Christ.
- Time to ponder upon current situations and how to make the best of them.

For the word of the Lord is truth, and whatsoever is truth is light, and whatsoever is light is Spirit, even the Spirit of Jesus Christ.

—Doctrine and Covenants 84:45

10. ANYTIME, ANYWHERE, ANYPLACE

Prepare an emergency talk or lesson to give at Church.

PURPOSE

To be prepared, if asked, to teach or speak with little or no notice.

PREPARATION

Choose a topic about which you possess a solid testimony. Prior to starting your evening, have all resources such as the scriptures, auxiliary manuals, copies of the *Ensign,* stories, and poems gathered in one place for easy access. Set out the presentation of your talk or lesson so that adaptations for length and various age groups are easy to apply.

POTENTIAL POSITIVE OUTCOMES

- An ability to convey a message with confidence during spur of the moment assignments.
- An opportunity to be quick to volunteer, thus rendering service, should the need for a substitute teacher/speaker arise.
- An opportunity to study the gospel now for yourself while meeting the needs of others in the future.

Let us cleanse ourselves from all filthiness of the flesh and spirit, perfecting holiness in the fear of God.

—2 Corinthians 7:1

11. LIVING IN RIGHTEOUSNESS

Go through all of your music (written and audio), books (including magazines and subscriptions), pictures, videos, and DVDs and throw away anything that does not measure up to the standards of the Church.

PURPOSE

To allow the Holy Ghost to always dwell in your home.

PREPARATION

More than physical preparation, this family home evening will require spiritual preparation. It will be up to you to determine, with the guidance of the Holy Ghost, where to draw the line between good and evil. During this cleansing process, there are no gray areas or room for justification. If in doubt, throw it out. Once your heart and mind are ready for this challenge, (for that's what it may be for some who truly want to make the best of this opportunity for growth), the physical part is easy. Gather ALL of the objects you need to sort through, leaving nothing on the shelf. Return only those that have the Spirit's approval.

POTENTIAL POSITIVE OUTCOMES

- An ability to make daily righteous decisions easily in regard to what you watch, listen to, or read.
- Commencement on the path to develop a lifelong habit of enjoying and pursuing virtuous entertainment.

- Determination to keep the commandments related to entertainment both inside and outside of your home.
- Establishment of a good example for those who come to your home.

But we can write a few words upon plates, which will give our children, and also our beloved brethren, a small degree of knowledge concerning us . . . hoping that our beloved brethren and our children will receive them with thankful hearts, and look upon them that they may learn with joy . . . that we knew of Christ . . . also all the holy prophets which were before us.

—Jacob 4:2–4

12. A RECORD FOR POSTERITY

Preserve your feelings about Jesus Christ, Joseph Smith and gospel principles for future generations.

PURPOSE

To have an account of your testimony for those who may need the assistance of your spiritual power after you have finished your mortal probation.

PREPARATION

Choose a method to preserve your testimony by voice recording, video taping, or writing, and organize the equipment needed. Through pondering and prayer, plan a brief outline of what you want to record and then let the Spirit guide you. Clearly label your testimony and store it in a secure place. Don't forget to make an extra copy and keep it in another location away from your home, just in case.

POTENTIAL POSITIVE OUTCOMES

- Evaluation of the relevance of your testimony in your own life.
- A uplifting source to which you can turn when you have need.
- Formation of a spiritual link between generations.

- Determination to live up to what you have recorded so that, after you are gone, your words may be believed and be of benefit to others.

Now behold, my brethren, I would ask if ye have read the scriptures?

—Alma 33:14

13. SUNDAY SCHOOL STUDY

Do the assigned Sunday School reading for the following Sunday.

PURPOSE

To be able to participate fully in this Church program regardless of your Sunday responsibilities.

PREPARATION

Obtain a copy of the current *Class Member Study Guide* from your Sunday school president or ward librarian. Find out the assignment for the next week's lesson and read the materials. If you are able to participate in class, write down questions to ask or comments to make about the lesson. If you are unable to attend each week, make arrangements with the teacher to get a copy of his notes to review.

POTENTIAL POSITIVE OUTCOMES

- Unity with the Sunday school class even if you're unable to personally participate with them.
- Inspiration from focussed gospel study.
- Satisfaction from fulfilling assignments to read and study the scriptures.

I will bless thee, and make thy name great.

—Genesis 12:2

14. A NAME AND A BLESSING

Review the blessing you received as a child, during which your name was officially recognized by the Church.

PURPOSE

To increase your knowledge of the potential Heavenly Father knows you have.

PREPARATION

First, determine whether a written record was made of your blessing and obtain a copy. If nothing was written, probe your parents' minds to see if they can remember anything, and ask family members to recall sacred memories of your early childhood. Read the materials and reflect on things that have come to pass. Make plans to fulfill or continue in obtaining promises that were mentioned in your blessing.

POTENTIAL POSITIVE OUTCOMES

- Further confirmation of your divinity as a child of God.
- Inspiration to continue in following the path that leads to exaltation.
- Knowledge about yourself that you may not have known before.

Lift up your heart and rejoice, for the hour of your mission is come; and your tongue shall be loosed, and you shall declare glad tidings of great joy unto this generation.

—Doctrine and Covenants 31:3

15. TWO SHORT YEARS

Write letters of support to all the people you know, young and old, who are serving full-time missions in any field.

PURPOSE

To sustain those who are sacrificing their time and talents in the name of Jesus Christ.

PREPARATION

Make a list of missionaries you know and be sure you have their correct addresses. Gather together stationery, appropriate postage stamps, pens, newspaper clippings, photographs, and anything else you may wish to include in your letters. Remember to keep the content appropriate for missionaries.

POTENTIAL POSITIVE OUTCOMES

- Missionaries are encouraged through your support.
- A desire to further your own missionary efforts.

I came not to judge the world, but to save the world.

—John 12:47

16. EASTER

Read the book of John in the New Testament.

PURPOSE

To come closer to Christ through the study of a specific book of scriptures about his life.

PREPARATION

Have your Bible, paper, marking pencils, and pens ready to use. Place a picture of the Savior nearby to help you concentrate as you learn, feel, and ponder. Prepare your heart to accept inspiration from the Holy Ghost to help you develop your testimony of Jesus Christ. Mark passages and write notes about scriptures that have special meaning to you at this time.

POTENTIAL POSITIVE OUTCOMES

- A renewed hope in the atonement of the Savior.
- An increased desire to be a dedicated follower of Christ.
- Appreciation for the Easter season beyond its commercialization.

And also to the convincing of the Jew and Gentile that Jesus is the Christ, the eternal God, manifesting himself unto all nations.

—Book of Mormon Title Page

17. PROCLAIM THE GOSPEL

Mark a copy of the Book of Mormon to give away to a friend.

PURPOSE

To dutifully proclaim the gospel as a mission of the Church.

PREPARATION

Obtain a copy of a new Book of Mormon from the full-time missionaries or your ward mission leader. With the help of the Holy Ghost, choose a friend, co-worker, acquaintance, or relative who may be receptive to the Book of Mormon. Once you have decided who the recipient will be, mark scriptures relevant to their interests, questions, and beliefs. You may want to ask the full-time missionaries to suggest possible scriptures. Finish by personally addressing the Book of Mormon to your friend and by writing your testimony. Pray for guidance on how to present the book so that it will be received in a positive light, and do so within the next seven days.

POTENTIAL POSITIVE OUTCOMES

- Accomplishment of missionary orientated goals.
- Development of your own testimony about the Book of Mormon.
- Planting gospel seeds in the lives if those you know.

Behold, will ye reject these words? Will ye reject the words of the prophets?

—Jacob 6:8

18. PRIESTHOOD OR RELIEF SOCIETY STUDY

Read the Priesthood or Relief Society lesson scheduled for the following Sunday's meetings.

PURPOSE

To deepen your understanding of gospel principles.

PREPARATION

Locate your current manual of study and find out what the next lesson scheduled is. Have marking pencils close at hand to highlight passages that have meaning to you. Jot down comments and questions that come to your mind. Use these notes to help you participate in the class on Sunday.

POTENTIAL POSITIVE OUTCOMES

- A realization that all lesson topics have relevance to you.
- Development of your testimony as you participate more fully in class.

I shall endeavour to write some of these things upon this record, for the benefit of my posterity that shall come after me.

—Abraham 1:31

19. JOURNAL ENTRIES

Write in your journal.

PURPOSE

To follow the counsel of President Spencer W. Kimball who said, "Every person should keep a journal and every person can keep a journal. If there is anyone here who isn't doing so, will you repent and change—change your life?" (Spencer W. Kimball, "Let Us Move Forward and Upward," *Ensign,* May 1979, 84).

PREPARATION

This activity is done in one of three different ways, depending on your personal manner of journal keeping.

1. If you have never or have seldom written in a journal, now is the time to start. Obtain a book in which you can record the events of your life. Don't worry about the past, but start recording the events of the day what you did, how you felt, who you saw, prayers that were answered, inspiration that came, your dreams, hopes, and anything else that comes to mind. Set a schedule to continue your record, occasionally including important past events.

2. If you have begun a journal but haven't written in it as frequently as you should, this evening is the time to catch up where you last left off. Take out your journal, start remembering, and start writing.

3. Daily journal writers obviously need no encouragement, so instead, dig out some old journals and read through them. Reminisce about the past and see how far you have come through former experiences.

POTENTIAL POSITIVE OUTCOMES

- Implementation of a righteous habit.
- Creation of a record for future generations to learn from.
- Remembrance of past experiences that may provide future strength and warning.

And it shall be given thee, also, to make a selection of sacred hymns, as it shall be given thee, which is pleasing unto me, to be had in my church.

—Doctrine and Covenants 25:11

20. MISSION MUSIC

Make a musical selection for a friend serving a full-time mission.

PURPOSE

To help a missionary feel closer to the Holy Ghost through appropriate sacred music.

PREPARATION

Contact the mission office where your friend is serving to find out the mission rules concerning personal music listening. Purchase a CD or cassette tape containing appropriate music for the missionary. Spend your evening listening to the music and write down the impressions you feel. Wrap the CD or tape and your notes, address the package, and send it within the week.

POTENTIAL POSITIVE OUTCOMES

- Creation of an environment where the Holy Ghost can dwell.
- Encouragement for missionaries laboring in the field.
- Expansion of your knowledge of available gospel music.

Seek ye out of the best books words of wisdom.

—Doctrine and Covenants 88:118

21. CHURCH LITERATURE

Spend the evening reading a Church book.

PURPOSE

To expand your knowledge of gospel principles.

PREPARATION

Obtain a copy of an inspirational book recommended by friends, the ward library, or from a Church book store. Sit back and relax as you become absorbed in feeling the Spirit through poring over words written by modern-day prophets, leaders, and inspired members of the Church.

POTENTIAL POSITIVE OUTCOMES

- Solidification of your testimony of the gospel.
- Answers to gospel questions.
- Motivation from the lives and experiences of others.

Lift up your head and be of good cheer; for behold, the time is at hand, and on this night shall the sign be given, and on the morrow come I into the world.

—3 Nephi 1:13

22. THE TRUE MEANING OF CHRISTMAS

Read chapters 1 and 2 from the book of Luke in the New Testament.

PURPOSE

To bring the Christmas season into the right perspective.

PREPARATION

Find your Bible. Have pictures of the Savior displayed while you read to help you concentrate. Have marking pencils, pens, and paper handy to make notes and mark inspirational passages. If it helps, play appropriate Christmas music in the background.

POTENTIAL POSITIVE OUTCOMES

- An increased testimony of the divinity of the Savior.
- Preservation of the true significance of Christmas.

Learn to impart one to another as the gospel requires.

—Doctrine and Covenants 88:123

23. SHARE YOUR EXPERIENCES

Write a response to the "Call for Articles" section of the *Ensign*.

PURPOSE

To uplift of your brothers and sisters in the gospel with your personal experiences.

PREPARATION

Watch for the "Call for Articles" printed several times a year in the *Ensign* for a topic for which you've had appropriate experience and can write about in an edifying way. Pray that the Holy Ghost will help you know what you to write. Spend the evening writing and rewriting, but be sure to carefully proofread and edit your article before submitting it, but do so promptly in order to be considered for publication.

POTENTIAL POSITIVE OUTCOMES

- Discovery of a purpose for some of life's experiences.
- Enhancement of your talent for writing.
- Encouragement for other members of the Church.

Jesus took bread, and blessed it, and brake it, and give it to the disciples.

—Matthew 26:26

24. THE SACRAMENTAL PRAYERS

Study and memorize Moroni 4:3 and 5:2.

PURPOSE

To deepen your testimony of the reality of the Atonement.

PREPARATION

All you need for this family home evening is your Book of Mormon and a heart ready to accept feelings from the Holy Ghost. Memorize the sacramental prayers. Look up all the scriptural cross references related to these scriptures. Ponder on what partaking of the sacrament means to you. Consider your worthiness and commitment to renew your baptismal covenant every week.

POTENTIAL POSITIVE OUTCOMES

- The significance if partaking of the sacrament becomes more evident in your life.
- A desire to live more worthy of the covenants you have made.

My heart pondereth continually upon the things which I have seen and heard.

—2 Nephi 4:16

25. VIDEO NIGHT

Watch a video or DVD produced by the Church.

PURPOSE

To feel the spirit and strengthen your testimony through available Church productions.

PREPARATION

If you do not own a VCR or DVD player, you need to invite yourself to someone's home who has one. From your own personal collection, the ward library or friends, select a Church video or DVD that will benefit you at this time.

POTENTIAL POSITIVE OUTCOMES

- Further insight into certain aspects of the gospel.
- Realization that Church productions are an alternative to watching those made for general entertainment.

For we have a labor to perform whilst in this tabernacle of clay.

—Moroni 9:6

26. GOALS

Set some long-term and short-term goals.

PURPOSE

To provide direction and meaning in your life.

PREPARATION

Decide on the scope of your goal-setting by concentrating on weekly or monthly goals, or plan for events ten years away. Be realistic and seek guidance from the Holy Ghost as you make your goals. Consult your patriarchal blessing for assistance. Once your goals have been set and written down, make a plan of action to achieve them. Display the goals in your home so that you are continuously focused on obtaining these righteous desires.

POTENTIAL POSITIVE OUTCOMES

- A worthwhile purpose in daily living.
- Guidance in reaching your ambitions.
- An elevation of self-worth as you achieve what you set out to do.

That there should be no iniquity among them.

—Moroni 6:7

27. EVEN THE LITTLE THINGS

Ponder upon all of the small things for which you need to repent and do so sincerely.

PURPOSE

To start a habit of daily repentance.

PREPARATION

Spiritual preparation for this activity is important. Look up scriptures on repentance and obtain copies of talks and articles written by Church leaders on the subject to read during the evening. As you pray and read, reflect on the changes you need to make in your life and write them down. Then perform the repentance necessary for you to be clean. Make this a daily practice.

POTENTIAL POSITIVE OUTCOMES

- An ability to live each day with a clear conscience.
- An increased testimony of repentance and the Atonement.
- A desire to live so that the necessity of repentance is minimal.
- An ability to help others thorough your personal experiences.
- Receptiveness to the promptings of the Holy Ghost made easier through your constant cleanliness and worthiness.

And I set my face unto the Lord God, to seek by prayer and supplications, with fasting.

—Daniel 9:3

28. THE LAW OF THE FAST

Fast for a particular reason.

PURPOSE

To increase your testimony of the power of fasting.

PREPARATION

Decide on a specific purpose for your fast, whether for yourself or someone else. Fast as you normally would during the day and end your fast as part of your family home evening. Previously determine what will help your fast be answered. Perhaps it will be just to pray some more. Prepare your fast offering slip as part of your evening. Once the envelope is sealed, place it where it will be easily found when you go to church the following week.

POTENTIAL POSITIVE OUTCOMES

- Answers to prayers.
- An increase of faith in the principle of fasting.
- An opportunity to be an instrument in assisting others during their trials and tribulations.
- An ability to bless the temporal lives of others through paying a generous fast offering.

It is the duty of the church . . . to support the families of those who are called and must needs be sent unto the world to proclaim the gospel unto the world.

—Doctrine and Covenants 75:24

29. CALLED TO SERVE

Provide an act of service for someone whose children or parents are serving a full-time mission.

PURPOSE

To show your gratitude for those sacrificing one hundred percent of their time to serve their God and fellow men.

PREPARATION

As all family situations are different, decide what form of service you will render to the family of the chosen missionary. Ideas include writing a letter expressing your appreciation for the efforts of their family member, anonymously delivering money to be put toward monthly mission payments, and making a parcel of stamps, envelopes, writing paper, and stickers for letters. Whatever you decide to do, ensure that you have what you need before you start your family home evening. If something needs to be delivered, do so as part of your activity.

POTENTIAL POSITIVE OUTCOMES

- An increased desire to do missionary work.
- Appreciation for the work loved ones are doing is felt by others.

And visit the house of each member, and exhort them to pray vocally and in secret and attend to all family duties.

—Doctrine and Covenants 20:47

30. MESSAGE OF LOVE

Prepare your home or visiting teaching message for the month.

PURPOSE

To have a relevant, spiritual message to share with those you have been assigned to visit.

PREPARATION

Locate a copy of the current month's *Ensign*. Be sensitive to the needs of those you visit as you prepare words of encouragement and wisdom. Make a list of any extra things you will need to take with you when you visit. Arrange a time to visit but avoid making these arrangements on a Monday night. You may want to invite your companion to share this family home evening with you.

POTENTIAL POSITIVE OUTCOMES

- An opportunity for the Holy Ghost to inform you of the needs of those you visit.
- An ability to share a message that has relevance and can be of assistance.
- Development of unity as brothers and sisters in the gospel.

And ye shall go forth in the power of my Spirit, preaching my gospel, two by two, in my name, lifting up your voices as with the sound of a trump, declaring my word like unto angels of God.

—Doctrine and Covenants 42:6

31. SACRIFICE

Spend your evening helping the full-time missionaries.

PURPOSE

To sacrifice your time to the building up of the kingdom of God.

PREPARATION

Contact the full-time missionaries serving in your area. Explain that on the night of their choosing, or the night of your family home evenings, you are at their disposal. They may ask you to visit less active members with them, hand out flyers, join in missionary discussions with those investigating the Church, cook them dinner, or mark copies of the Book of Mormon with your testimony. Whatever they ask, be ready and willing to do it.

POTENTIAL POSITIVE OUTCOMES

- An opportunity to help convert lives to the gospel of Jesus Christ.
- An increased desire to make missionary work a part of your daily life.

I have no greater joy then to hear that my children walk in truth.

—3 John 1:4

32. FUTURE LEADERS

Volunteer to organize a primary sharing time activity.

PURPOSE

To influence the lives of children around you for good.

PREPARATION

Contact the primary President in your ward and ask if you can help. If so, find out the monthly primary theme, ages and numbers of children, and their interests. Set a date to present your sharing time. Spend the evening obtaining the materials you will need, organizing the information, and preparing a spiritual and exciting sharing time activity.

POTENTIAL POSITIVE OUTCOMES

- An opportunity to touch the lives of the children in your ward.
- An opportunity to help the primary presidency in their calling to teach the gospel to future leaders of the Church.

Therefore all things whatsoever ye would that men should do to you, do ye even so to them.

—Matthew 7:12

33. PERFECTION

Make a list of the qualities you desire in an eternal companion and then make plans to improve those attributes in your own life.

PURPOSE

To be worthy to enter into the new and everlasting covenant of marriage.

PREPARATION

A pen, a piece of paper, and a heart receptive to the Holy Ghost is all you need for this family home evening. Sincerely think about the characteristics of a person with whom you would like to spend eternity. List these characteristics with the reasons why they are important for eternal happiness. Honestly evaluate the development of these qualities in your own character. Set self-improvement goals in those areas that need a little work.

POTENTIAL POSITIVE OUTCOMES

- Knowledge of marriage as an eternal principle.
- Reservation of judgement toward those who are also not yet perfect.
- Formation of clear standards for yourself and others with whom you may form intimate relationships.
- An opportunity to progress in your own goals.

And we did magnify our office unto the Lord.

—Jacob 1:19

34. SERVICE IN THE KINGDOM OF GOD

Spend the evening doing something to magnify your church calling.

PURPOSE

To fulfill the responsibilities which Heavenly Father has entrusted to you at this time.

PREPARATION

Decide what you need to do to improve in your calling. Organize any materials that you will need to accomplish what you plan to do. This is not an evening to feel guilty because you've not been doing everything you should; rather, it's a wonderful opportunity to get back on top of things, to renew your zeal in doing what you have been commissioned to by God.

POTENTIAL POSITIVE OUTCOMES

- Enrichment of the lives of all those influenced by your position in the Church.
- An increased motivation to continue to magnify your callings.

But, notwithstanding the greatness of the task, I must do according to the strict commands of God.

—Jacob 2:10

35. ONE HUNDRED PERCENT

Choose a gospel principle with which you have difficulty and prepare to live it perfectly for the next seven days.

PURPOSE

To begin a righteous practice that will last a lifetime.

PREPARATION

Take an honest look at your commitment to living gospel principles and choose an area that needs improvement. On the night of your family home evening, read relevant scriptures, *Ensign* articles, and listen to the promptings of the Holy Ghost to form a plan that will enable you to be one hundred percent obedient. Start to implement your plan immediately. Evaluate your progress at the end of the week and continue your efforts until you feel comfortable.

POTENTIAL POSITIVE OUTCOMES

- Recognition of the blessings that come from obedience.
- An opportunity to repent and gain knowledge that you have been forgiven.
- Motivation to improve in keeping other commandments.

Wherefore, we search the prophets.

—Jacob 4:6

36. FOR OUR TIME

Learn more about the life of the prophet chosen for the current year of study in Relief Society and Priesthood meetings.

PURPOSE

To increase your testimony of the divinity of this prophet.

PREPARATION

Obtain books, cassette tapes, CDs, videos, DVDs, pictures, and magazines in which the prophet appears as author or subject. Because you may accumulate a large number of resources, select those pieces that are of most interest to you. Envelop yourself in the life of this man as you listen to, watch, and read about him during your family home evening.

POTENTIAL POSITIVE OUTCOMES

- An increased love and respect for this prophet.
- A desire to participate more fully in your Relief Society and Priesthood meetings.
- Direction and inspiration in your life through your study.

Hearken, O ye house of Israel, and hear the words of me, a prophet of the Lord.

—Jacob 5:2

37. GENERAL CONFERENCE

Review messages from the latest General Conference of the Church.

PURPOSE

To keep fresh in your mind relevant warnings and directions for today from inspired sisters and brethren.

PREPARATION

General Conference is available in the *Ensign* and *Liahona* magazines, videos and DVDs, or on the Internet. Decide which media best suits your circumstances. Arrange to borrow these resources, through your ward library, if necessary. Use your family home evening to study the messages that have special interest for you.

POTENTIAL POSITIVE OUTCOMES

- An awareness of what Heavenly Father would have you do right now.
- Remembrance of the feelings of the spirit you felt when you first heard these messages.

Now the sons of Jacob were twelve.

—Genesis 35:22

38. THE TWELVE TRIBES OF ISRAEL

Search the scriptures that make reference to the tribe of Israel revealed in your patriarchal blessing.

PURPOSE

To increase your testimony of your worth and identity.

PREPARATION

If you have not received your patriarchal blessing, first follow lesson one, "Just For You," in the Spiritual Focus section. For those already in possession of a patriarchal blessing, look up all the scriptures in the Topical Guide that refer to the tribe of your lineage. Have a pen, paper, and marking pencils ready to write down any inspired thoughts or mark interesting passages of scripture.

POTENTIAL POSITIVE OUTCOMES

- An increased reality and importance of your lineage.
- Preparation to receive the blessings associated with your tribe as you learn what they are.

Now behold, I, Jarom, write a few words according to the commandment of my father, Enos, that our genealogy may be kept.

—Jarom 1:1

39. FOUR GENERATIONS

"We want to emphasize again and place squarely upon the shoulders of these individuals and their families the obligation to complete the four-generation program" (Spencer W. Kimball, "The True Way of Life and Salvation," *Ensign*, May 1978, 4).

PURPOSE

To obey the commandments of God given through His prophet.

PREPARATION

Obtain a four-generation sheet from your ward family history consultant or Church Distribution Center. Seek out the information you need to complete the sheet from your relatives, on the Internet, and at family history centers. You may like to combine this family home evening with lesson seven of the Spiritual Focus section, "Family History? Help!" As you are filling in all the data on the sheet, reflect on the lives of your ancestors. If available, display photographs or other memorabilia of your ancestors around your home while you work on this project. Even if your parents have completed their sheets, it's essential for you to have your own copy. Keep this record in a secure place. If you are the first person in your family to begin family history work, talk to your ward family history consultant about further steps to take so that your progenitors can enjoy the blessings of the gospel of Jesus Christ.

POTENTIAL POSITIVE OUTCOMES

- Commencement of your own family history efforts.
- Qualification to receive blessings that come from obedience to prophetic instruction.
- Salvation for those beyond the veil made possible.

Six days shall thy work be done, but on the seventh day there shall be to you an holy day, a sabbath of rest to the Lord.

—Exodus 35:2

40. THE SABBATH DAY

Set personal standards for honoring the Lord's day.

PURPOSE

To qualify for the blessings that come from obeying the commandment to keep the Sabbath day holy.

PREPARATION

During your family home evening, read through all of the scriptures associated with Sabbath day observances. From what you read, list all that is required of you on this day. With the help of the Holy Ghost, translate these into modern day terms and create specific guidelines to which you can refer. Remember to include both the things you should do as well as those things that you should avoid. Place this list in your home and consult it regularly so that you are ready to implement it every Sunday.

POTENTIAL POSITIVE OUTCOMES

- An ability to follow this commandment clearly and easily.
- Appreciation for the Sabbath as a true day of service, rest and spiritual growth.

Were it not for these plates, which contain these records and these commandments, we must have suffered in ignorance, even at this present time, not knowing the mysteries of God.

—Mosiah 1:3

41. A SACRED RECORD

Begin a study of the Book of Mormon.

PURPOSE

To strengthen your testimony of the Book of Mormon and recognize its personal value.

PREPARATION

Obtain a new, unmarked, inexpensive copy of the Book of Mormon. Decide on the approach you will take in this study of the Book of Mormon. Possible methods to consider are reading from cover to cover marking off chapters as you finish each one, using Sunday School, Seminary, or Institute manuals for reference as you read, reading through chronologically, or taking a thematic approach such as marking all passages referring to Christ. Obtain the materials you will need for whichever technique you choose. After starting during family home evening, make a goal to continue your study on a daily basis.

POTENTIAL POSITIVE OUTCOMES

- Creating an avenue through which the Holy Ghost can communicate with you.
- Discovering new insights from the Book of Mormon that you had not previously recognized.
- Daily strength from feasting on the words of God.

So many of the blessings were poured out upon the people, that even the high priests and the teachers were themselves astonished beyond measure.

—Helaman 3:25

42. COUNT YOUR BLESSINGS

Make a list of all the temporal and spiritual blessings you have received.

PURPOSE

To strengthen your testimony of the personal involvement of God in your life.

PREPARATION

All you need for this evening is a pen, a piece of paper, and a heart ready to recognize all that God has given you. You may want to divide your list into categories. For example: educational blessings, work blessings, church blessings, family blessings, and friendship blessings. Make neat copies of your list and place them in various positions around your home—on your refrigerator, in your scriptures, or near where you pray, as a constant reminder of all your blessings. Add to these lists as you receive more blessings. Remember to thank Heavenly Father for all these blessings as you close your family home evening.

POTENTIAL POSITIVE OUTCOMES

- A realization of just how many blessings you do have.
- A source of reference when speaking words of gratitude to your Father in Heaven.
- A place to turn when you are feeling low, thus receiving encouragement to obtain additional blessings.

Will ye give to an humble servant of God something to eat?

—Alma 8:19

43. SERVANTS OF THE LORD

Invite the full-time missionaries serving in your area over for a meal.

PURPOSE

To support the missionary program of the Church.

PREPARATION

Invite the missionaries to eat with you. Find out what foods they like and dislike. Ask them to share a spiritual message with you. Keep the length of the visit to within the time frame specified by the mission rules. If you are a single sister inviting the elders, you will need to invite other friends to share this meal with you and the missionaries.

POTENTIAL POSITIVE OUTCOMES

- Qualification for blessings given to those who serve those on the Lord's errand.
- An increased desire to do missionary work.
- Formation of friendships.

And he hath put a new song in my mouth, even praise unto our God.

—Psalm 40:3

44. SACRED MUSIC

Write a new verse to your favorite hymn or write a new hymn.

PURPOSE

To express your feelings about the Savior through music.

PREPARATION

Obtain a copy of *Hymns of The Church of Jesus Christ of Latter-day Saints* and identify your favorite hymn. Familiarize yourself with its tune and lyrics. Have a pen and paper handy. Start by writing a brief testimony about the theme of the hymn. Using what you write as a guide, follow the pattern of the hymn to write a new verse. Consider the rhyming and repetition pattern of various lines. Continuously sing to yourself what you are writing, and finally sing the whole hymn through to check to see if your verse flows with the printed hymn. Remember that your verse may fit at the beginning, the middle or the end. Paste a copy of your new verse in your hymnal or scriptures. When appropriate, sing the new verse whenever you sing your favoritc hymn.

POTENTIAL POSITIVE OUTCOMES

- Appreciation for those who have written, and continue to write, sacred hymns.
- Expression of your testimony through putting your feelings to music.

And the words which I have written in weakness will be made strong unto them; for it persuadeth them to do good; it maketh known unto them of their fathers; and it speaketh of Jesus, and persuadeth them to believe in him, and to endure to the end, which is life eternal.

—2 Nephi 33:4

45. A DAILY REMINDER

Select one or two scriptures as your theme for the coming year.

PURPOSE

To have sacred words become a focus and guide for you in your daily life.

PREPARATION

Think about where you would like to be and what you would like to accomplish within the next twelve months. Ponder upon what spiritual motivation will be helpful to you in achieving your desires. Search the scriptures to find a verse or two that will be a constant inspiration to you on a daily basis. Have large pieces of paper handy on which to write or type these scriptures. Display them in a prominent place in your home and read them every day.

POTENTIAL POSITIVE OUTCOMES

- Guidance from the Holy Ghost through reading the scriptures.
- A continuous reminder of the potential you have and how it can be reached.
- Daily assistance in keeping temporal and spiritual perspectives of life.

My son, peace be unto thy soul; thine adversity and afflictions shall be but a small moment; and then, if thou endure it well, God shall exalt thee on high; thou shalt triumph over all thy foes.

—Doctrine and Covenants 121:7–8

46. SUCCESSFUL ENDURANCE

Ponder the trials you have faced in your life and reflect on what you learned from them.

PURPOSE

To find the positive in any situation.

PREPARATION

Purchase a new notebook or journal for this activity and have pens handy. During your family home evening, reflect on some of the larger challenges you have dealt with throughout your life. Write them in your notebook. Using hindsight and the Holy Ghost, ponder the spiritual and temporal lessons you have learned from your trials, and write these in your notebook. Keep this record in an accessible place. Frequently refer to it when your are experiencing hardships, having trouble seeing the brighter side of life, or want reassurance that God has a purpose for you. Update your adversity notebook on a regular basis.

POTENTIAL POSITIVE OUTCOMES

- Peace, as you discover the reasons you have experienced trials.
- An ability to face future afflictions with a more determined attitude to conquer them because you know you have previously been successful.

- An increased testimony that God knows you and allows things to happen so that you can reach your potential.
- A tangible resource to help you keep things in perspective.

And again, verily I say unto you, if a man marry a wife by my word, which is my law, and by the new and everlasting covenant, and it is sealed unto them by the Holy Spirit of promise, by him who is anointed, unto whom I have appointed this power and the keys of this priesthood; and it shall be said unto them—Ye shall come forth in the first resurrection . . . and shall inherit thrones, kingdoms, principalities, and powers, dominions, all heights and depth.

—Doctrine and Covenants 132:19

47. PREPARING FOR ETERNITY

Make a collection of articles written by members of the Church about marriage relationships.

PURPOSE

To have a resource of righteous advice and tips on marriage to study now and put into practice in the future.

PREPARATION

There are a couple ways to gather articles from the *Ensign* magazine: the *LDS Church Magazines 1971–1999* CD-ROM or logging onto www.lds.org. Decide how you will preserve the articles you find. Organizational ideas include pasting them into a scrapbook, filing them under different themes, or binding them together to form your own book. Obtain what you need to store the articles before you begin your family home evening. Don't forget to include the names and dates of magazines, books, or articles used if they are not on your printed copies. Continuously update your collection from current *Ensign* magazines and lessons given at Church.

POTENTIAL POSITIVE OUTCOMES

- Cultivation of thoughts focussed on the true meaning and purpose of a temple marriage and eternal goals.
- Knowledge and counsel from correct and true sources about love and relationships.

Now they were ordained after this manner—being called with a holy calling, and ordained with a holy ordinance . . . and it was on account of their exceeding faith and repentance, and their righteousness before God.

—Alma 13:8, 10

48. THE HOLY PRIESTHOOD OF GOD

Make or buy a gift for a young man in your family or ward who is about to advance in the priesthood.

PURPOSE

To let the youth of the Church know the respect you have for priesthood authority.

PREPARATION

For this family home evening, prepare a small parcel for a young man to and give it to him on the day of his priesthood advancement. This parcel could include a letter of gratitude to the young man for his worthiness to progress, a copy of your testimony about the restoration of the priesthood and its significance in your life, a new copy of the Book of Mormon, a tie, or an oil vial for those receiving the Melchizedek Priesthood. Organize these things, along with a congratulatory card during the family home evening the Monday before the young man will be ordained.

POTENTIAL POSITIVE OUTCOMES

- Encouragement for those who hold the priesthood to always remain worthy to do so.
- An increased testimony of the priesthood.
- Creation and nourishment of friendships.

God does inspire men and call them to his holy work in this age and generation, as well as in generations of old.

—Doctrine and Covenants 20:11

49. PSALMS AND PROVERBS

Write a poem about an aspect of the gospel.

PURPOSE

To express your testimony through poetic verse.

PREPARATION

Choose a theme for your poem and the style in which you feel comfortable writing. You may wish to spend time at your local library or on the internet researching various styles of poetry. With a prayer in your heart, write down the feelings you have for the gospel. Once you have a rough draft, read and reread your poem making alterations as necessary. Your poem, may only be two lines, or it may be two pages. Once you have completed your poem, file it away to use in a lesson, talk, or visiting or home teaching message. You may also keep a copy in your scriptures.

POTENTIAL POSITIVE OUTCOMES

- An increased testimony as you put your feelings into words.
- Discovery of a new skill or talent.
- Recognition of the influence of the Holy Ghost as he inspires you while you write your poem.

Wherefore, be not weary in well-doing, for ye are laying the foundation of a great work.

—Doctrine and Covenants 64:33

50. FAMILY HOME EVENING FOLDER

Collect family home evening ideas from the *Ensign* that have been printed over the last number of years.

PURPOSE

To build a valuable resource for future family home evenings.

PREPARATION

If you do not keep copies of the *Ensign,* ask members of your ward for any back issues they no longer wish to use. You may also log onto www.lds.org. Click on Gospel Library and go to the Church Publications—HTML or PDF section. Spend your evening reading through the family home evening ideas that are usually located toward the back of the *Ensign.* Cut out or print off any ideas that are of particular interest to you. Decide how you will organize and store these ideas. Don't forget to include the names and dates of articles used of they are not printed on your copies. Plan to check each month's *Ensign* from now on for more family home evening ideas to add to your collection.

POTENTIAL POSITIVE OUTCOMES

- A resource of family home evening ideas to help you through all stages of life.
- An increased enthusiasm to hold family home evening through the motivation of others.

- Growth of your testimony of the importance of family home evening.
- Appreciation for those who put their time into sharing their ideas in the Ensign.

And this shall be our covenant—that we will walk in all the ordinances of the Lord.

—Doctrine and Covenants 136:4

51. A COVENANT PEOPLE

Review the covenants you have made with God up until this point in your life.

PURPOSE

To increase your awareness of the sacred promises you have made with deity.

PREPARATION

You will need your scriptures, a copy of your patriarchal blessing, journal entries of when you made sacred covenants, copies of doctrinal Church books, paper, and a pen. During your family home evening, list all the covenants that you have made in your life thus far. With the help of your collected resources, write down all that you have covenanted to do and how Heavenly Father will bless you in return. Evaluate the standard of success you are achieving in keeping these promises you have made. Read your journal entries about the feelings you had at the time you made covenants with God. Ponder what changes you need to make in your life to fulfill those covenants on a higher level; there's always room for improvement. Make plans to do so and pray for help.

POTENTIAL POSITIVE OUTCOMES

- Remembrance of all that you have promised to do.
- Improvement of your relationship with Christ as you commit to follow him more zealously.
- Further assistance from the heavens as you become more worthy to enter the presence of God.

We believe in God, the Eternal Father, and in His Son, Jesus Christ, and in the Holy Ghost.

—Articles of Faith 1:1

52. WE BELIEVE

Memorize the Articles of Faith.

PURPOSE

To solidify your knowledge of basic gospel principles.

PREPARATION

All you need for this family home evening is a quiet place with no distractions and your scriptures. Spend your time memorizing the Articles of Faith found in the Pearl of Great Price. Looking up the cross-referenced scriptures will complement your study. Frequently review the Articles of Faith and ponder their meaning in your life as part of your personal scripture study.

POTENTIAL POSITIVE OUTCOMES

- An increased testimony of gospel principles and doctrines.
- Preparation to answer questions about the Church at any time.
- An increased testimony of Joseph Smith and his role in the restoration of the gospel in these latter days.

And that same sociality which exists among us here will exist among us there, only it will be coupled with eternal glory, which glory we do not now enjoy.

—Doctrine and Covenants 130:2

Section 2: Social Focus

AN IDEA FOR EVERY WEEK OF THE YEAR

But the stranger that dwelleth with you shall be unto you as one born among you, and thou shalt love him as thyself.

—Leviticus 19:34

1. WELCOME

Invite a new individual or family in your ward or neighborhood to your home for family home evening.

PURPOSE

To strengthen friendships with those you do not know so well.

PREPARATION

Select the individual or family you would like to invite and set a date for your family home evening with them. Find out all you can, in an interested and genuine way, about their likes and dislikes, family situation, and talents. From what you learn, plan an appropriate family home evening that will allow everyone to feel comfortable. Assign them to participate in bringing the treat or saying the opening or closing prayer. Take care not to make the assignment something that may cause your guests to feel awkward. If you have a shy disposition, invite other people that you know well to join you.

POTENTIAL POSITIVE OUTCOMES

- Creation of new friendships.
- The introduction of the family home evening program to those who may not know of its wonderful benefits.

We believe in being subject to kings, presidents, rulers and magistrates, in obeying, honoring, and sustaining the law.

—Articles of Faith 1:12

2. CITIZENS OF EXAMPLE

Choose an area of your local law to live one hundred percent correctly.

PURPOSE

To be obedient to the laws of the land.

PREPARATION

Ponder if there are laws that you are not living to the letter. Perhaps you creep over the speed limit, don't always cross the road at designated points, share a plate from the salad bar when you only paid for one, use your cell phone while driving, or don't always wear your seat belt. Resolve to change your habits and make a plan by which you can always follow the laws that have been established in your land. If you're not sure about a specific law, then research it. Resolve to obey your designated law until it becomes a habit.

POTENTIAL POSITIVE OUTCOMES

- A clear conscience as you live as a responsible member of your community.
- Resistance to temptations to break further laws.
- An ability to set a good example or others.
- Awareness for the need to make your society a better place to live.

Despise not thy mother when she is old.

—Proverbs 23:22

3. MOTHER'S DAY

Show your gratitude to your mother or a woman in your life who has played a similar role.

PURPOSE

To appreciate, as Sheri L. Dew has stated, "What the doctrine of motherhood means for *all* of us" (Sheri L. Dew, "Are We Not All Mothers?" *Ensign,* November 2001, 96).

PREPARATION

Hold this family home evening the week before Mother's Day. Decide on who you want to honor and organize what you will need to prepare a simple gift for this person. It could be a thank you letter, something handmade, a purchase that has significant meaning, or any other way you feel comfortable showing your love. Make arrangements to give your gift on Mother's Day.

POTENTIAL POSITIVE OUTCOMES

- An opportunity to think about the good women who have blessed your life.
- Motivation to follow the example of righteous women and acknowledge their significant role in the Plan of Salvation.

And I would that ye should remember, that whosoever among you borroweth of his neighbor should return the thing that he borroweth.

—Mosiah 4:28

4. HONESTY IS THE BEST POLICY

Find things you have borrowed, no matter how long ago, and make plans to return them.

PURPOSE

To improve your effort to be more honest in your dealings with your fellow men.

PREPARATION

No preparation is necessary for this activity apart from building up the courage to return things to their rightful owners. Go through your closets and bookshelves and ferret out everything that you have borrowed whether recently or ten years ago. Make preparations to return all the items you borrowed within the next seven days. Wrap the items needing to be returned by mail. Begin to return the other items in person on your family home evening.

POTENTIAL POSITIVE OUTCOMES

- Procrastination and dishonesty are overcome.
- Formation of a habit to be prompt in your return of borrowed goods.

To clothe the naked, and to feed the hungry, and to liberate the captive, and administer relief to the sick and afflicted.

—Jacob 2:19

5. THE WELFARE OF OTHERS

Provide some service to someone in your ward.

PURPOSE

To help give temporal relief to the needy in your ward.

PREPARATION

Explain your purpose for this activity to a member of the ward welfare council, being aware that you don't need to receive confidential or sensitive information but decide how you are best able to assist. Arrange everything you may need, including purchasing food or clothing. Sort out these items from your own closets that you can donate, buy ingredients to make a meal, and arrange for transport to deliver things. On your family home evening night put everything together and set about delivering it. If anonymity is needed, drop your donation on the doorstep with an explanatory note and ring the doorbell. If you intend to visit, schedule an appointment beforehand.

POTENTIAL POSITIVE OUTCOMES

- A broader perspective about the lives of those around you.
- Gratitude for the temporal blessings you have.
- Nourishment of friendships.
- Approval from Christ as you follow his example of love.

Think of your brethren like unto yourself, and be familiar with all and free of your substance, that they may be rich like unto you.
—Jacob 2:17

6. CHARITABLE DONATIONS

Sort through your clothes and other items, selecting goods to donate to a charity of your choice.

PURPOSE

To help give temporal relief to the needy in your community.

PREPARATION

Decide upon which charitable organization to donate your items. If appropriate, call and ask what their most needed items are at this time. During your family home evening, gather together belongings that you no longer need which are still in reasonably good condition. Make arrangements to deliver them within the next seven days.

POTENTIAL POSITIVE OUTCOMES

- Responsibly recycling unwanted items to benefit others.
- An increased understanding of the lives of others in your community.
- Appreciation for the temporal blessings you have.

But I say unto you, That whosoever is angry with is brother shall be in danger of the judgement.

—JST Matthew 5:22

7. BEAR NO MALICE

Make peace with someone by apologizing about a past misunderstanding.

PURPOSE

To be able to enjoy lasting peace and help others to do so as well.

PREPARATION

Think and pray about people who have offended you or you may have offended. Decide what you can do to repair the damage that has been caused to your relationship. You may need to write a letter, make a phone call, or arrange a personal visit. Sincerely and honestly wanting to make amends will be the best preparation you can make for this family home evening.

POTENTIAL POSITIVE OUTCOMES

- Restoration of friendships which are strengthened as you resolve misunderstandings.
- A desire to address problems of this nature with quicker and more positive action in the future.

For how knoweth a man the master whom he has not served, and who is a stranger unto him, and is far from the thoughts and intents of his heart?

—Mosiah 5:13

8. SERVE THY MASTER

Do something nice for your employer.

PURPOSE

To be an example of Christ through service.

PREPARATION

Spend the week before this family home evening paying particular attention to the character and schedule of your boss. Decide on an act of service you can do, anonymous or otherwise, to ease the burdens of this person. Have everything you need to carry out this deed on your family home evening night. Event if you are not employed, this family home evening still applies. Select a teacher, student, acquaintance, or friend to serve.

POTENTIAL POSITIVE OUTCOMES

- Nourishment of friendships.
- Appreciation for the efforts of others as you focus on their needs.

He was desirous to know concerning the people who went up to dwell in the land of Lehi-Nephi . . . for his people had heard nothing from them from the time they left.

—Mosiah 7:1

9. LONG LOST FRIENDS

Contact a friend who you have not heard from in a long time.

PURPOSE

To renew past friendships.

PREPARATION

Reflect on your school days, past wards or neighborhoods, places of employment, and sporting clubs. Write down names of those people with whom you used to know and select a few of those people to whom you were quite close. Spend your family home evening finding out contact information, if necessary, and then get in touch with them by calling on the telephone, writing a letter, visiting, or sending an e-mail.

POTENTIAL POSITIVE OUTCOMES

- Renewal of relationships with those who were a positive influence in your life.

And now, behold, I give unto you a commandment, that when ye are assembled together ye shall instruct and edify each other.

—Doctrine and Covenants 43:8

10. MAKE YOURSELF AT HOME

Invite yourself to a friend's home for family home evening.

PURPOSE

To experience how others live the gospel through family home evening.

PREPARATION

Prayerfully select a family or individual with whom you are comfortable, and ask to spend a family home evening with them. Offer to provide the lesson, a treat, a musical number, or another part of the evening's activities and make sure that your part is well-prepared.

POTENTIAL POSITIVE OUTCOMES

- Enjoyment of family home evening in the company of good friends.
- Acquisition of new ideas to enhance your own family home evenings now and in the future.
- Growth together in the gospel.

Therefore, all things whatsoever ye would that men should do to you, do ye even so to them.

—3 Nephi 4:12

11. SURPRISE!

Throw a surprise party for someone.

PURPOSE

To let others know that you love and appreciate them.

PREPARATION

Select a person for whom you'd like to throw a surprise party and the occasion you wish to celebrate such as a birthday, graduation, engagement, farewell, or other specific accomplishment. You may want to use the family home evening night leading up to this to prepare invitations, games, and decorations. Depending on the number of guests you invite, you may need to find a place for the party outside your home. Be sure to follow up with food and other assignments a few days before the party.

POTENTIAL POSITIVE OUTCOMES

- Development of friendships.
- Encouragement for others to have and enjoy family home evening.

The glory of children are their fathers.

—Proverbs 17:6

12. FATHER'S DAY

Do something to express your love for your earthly father.

PURPOSE

To show your appreciation for the life of your father or other important men in your life.

PREPARATION

If your father is no longer living, you may want to replace this with lesson forty-seven, "Respect for the Dead," in the Temporal Focus section. If you have a living father—whether he be your dad, grandfather, father-in-law, or great friend and adviser—think about what you can do to make the Fathers' Day memorable for him. Organize all you'll need in advance and spend your evening preparing for and making your father feel like the most important man in the world.

POTENTIAL POSITIVE OUTCOMES

- A continuation of love for your father.
- An increase of your testimony of eternal families
- Blessings that come from showing gratitude.

And plant gardens, and eat the fruit of them.

—Jeremiah 29:5

13. HARVEST SEASON

Go fruit-picking.

PURPOSE

To enjoy the variety of good foods that God has created for you.

PREPARATION

This will be a seasonal family home evening, so learn what fruits are available in your area, through word-of-mouth, television, newspaper, Internet, and other advertisements. Make an appointment to go pick, perhaps inviting friends and family members to join you. You may want to pick extra fruit to share with others or preserve for your own use. (See lesson thirty-seven, "Never Hunger," in the Temporal Focus section.)

POTENTIAL POSITIVE OUTCOMES

- Appreciation for the creations of Heavenly Father and his son.
- Satisfaction that comes from laboring in the out-of-doors.
- Gratitude for the healthy food available to eat.

I write unto you again that ye may know that I am yet alive.
—Moroni 9:1

14. KEEPING IN TOUCH

Write a newsletter about the last twelve months of your life to send to friends and relatives living far from you.

PURPOSE

The strengthen long-distance relationships.

PREPARATION

Gather together your journal entries, photos, and calendar from the last twelve months. Put together a newsletter including details about achievements, holidays, changes, callings, hopes, relationships, and your testimony. If you plan to mass produce this for numerous friends and family members make arrangements for copying. Have the appropriate postage, envelopes, and addresses ready, and send your newsletter within the next seven days. Keep a copy to add to your own personal history. Plan to make this an annual family home evening, but it does not need to be done during the busy Christmas season.

POTENTIAL POSITIVE OUTCOMES

- Enjoyable reflection on the past year of your life and what you have achieved.
- Development of relationships regardless of physical separation.

Everyman according as he purposeth in his heart, so let him give; not grudgingly, or of necessity: for God loveth a cheerful giver.

—2 Corinthians 9:7

15. WARM FOOD AND A WARM HEART

Cook a meal to take to your neighbor.

PURPOSE

To offer service to those in your neighborhood.

PREPARATION

Decide which neighbor you wish to serve and, if possible, find out what food he likes and dislikes. You may present the meal as a surprise or tell him in advance that you'll be providing the meal. Choose recipes and purchase the ingredients before that night. Be sure to make enough for the entire household and prepare it to deliver at an early mealtime on your family home evening.

POTENTIAL POSITIVE OUTCOMES

- Improvement of your homemaking skills.
- Reduction of burdens in the lives of others.
- Development of neighborhood relationships.

Having been born of goodly parents.

—1 Nephi 1:1

16. CONGRATULATIONS

Give a present to someone you know who's had a baby.

PURPOSE

To add joy to the lives of your friends.

PREPARATION

Stay alert to the condition of mothers who are expecting babies in your ward, family, or neighborhood. Purchase a collection of small needed baby items and wrapping paper. On your family home evening, wrap your package and deliver it to the home or hospital (after checking to see if the new mother is ready for visitors). You might like to include your testimony in a card about the wonderful responsibility of raising the spirit children of our Heavenly Father as part of your present.

POTENTIAL POSITIVE OUTCOMES

- An increased testimony of the premortal world.
- Development of friendships.

I was sick, and ye visited me.

—Matthew 25:36

17. THE SICK AND THE NEEDY

Visit someone you know who is in the hospital.

PURPOSE

To cheek those with physical ailments.

PREPARATION

Be aware of those in your ward, family, or neighborhood who are ill. Talk to the sick person's family or close friends to determine the best time to visit. Obtain the hospital name, room number, visiting hours, and any visiting restriction information. You may wish to prepare a small gift, if you feel it is appropriate. Be prepared to have a positive, fun visit no matter what the circumstances.

POTENTIAL POSITIVE OUTCOMES

- Physical and perhaps emotional and spiritual burdens of others are lifted.

So yes shall not pollute the land wherein ye are.

—Numbers 35:33

18. A PLEASING ENVIRONMENT

Spend the evening picking up litter around your neighborhood.

PURPOSE

To help keep the Earth a beautiful place to live.

PREPARATION

Invite a few friends to join you for this family home evening. A few weeks before, take special note of areas around your neighborhood such as parks, bus stops, parking lots, beaches, and school yards that are prone to becoming littered. Provide waterproof gloves and garbage bags available as you go through the places you've located and pick up the garbage. If you come across hazardous materials, mark them and call the appropriate authority the following day. You may wish to obtain this phone number as part of your family home evening preparation to make contacting them easier.

POTENTIAL POSITIVE OUTCOMES

- Fulfillment of your responsibility to care for the earth which God has made.
- An awareness of pollution and damage that litter can cause to the environment.
- A positive example for those in your neighborhood to follow.

For unto us a child is born, unto us a son is given: and the government shall be upon his shoulder: and his name shall be called Wonderful, Counsellor, The mighty God, The everlasting Father, The Prince of Peace.

—Isaiah 9:6

19. BLESSED BE HIS NAME

Go Christmas carolling.

PURPOSE

To help others feel the spirit of Christmas through song.

PREPARATION

Gather together friends and relatives to join you for this family home evening. Decide where, when, and the duration of your caroling. Possible venues include your neighborhood, less-active members' homes, retirement homes, hospitals, or orphanages. Contact the relevant people for permission to sing at the locale of your choice. Arrange a practice or two before your family home evening and have hymn or song books ready to use.

POTENTIAL POSITIVE OUTCOMES

- Appropriate focus on the true meaning of Christmas.
- Development of friendships and hope through the teachings of Christ.

Live joyfully with the wife whom thou lovest.

—Ecclesiastes 9:9

20. DATE NIGHT

Babysit for a couple in your ward, for free, so they can enjoy an evening alone together.

PURPOSE

To help strengthen the marriages of others.

PREPARATION

Prayerfully choose a couple in your ward or neighborhood who could benefit from this service. Discuss with them a date and time for you to help. Before they leave, make sure that you have the necessary information regarding emergency contacts, children's allergies or special needs. Carry out any instruction given by the parents. Relax and enjoy yourself.

POTENTIAL POSITIVE OUTCOMES

- A glimpse into what may lie ahead in your life.
- An increased testimony of eternal families.
- Development of relationship skills with people of all ages.

Glory to God in the highest, and on earth peace, good will toward men.

—Luke 2:14

21. TWELVE DAYS OF CHRISTMAS

Leave surprise gifts in the doorstep of a friend's home for the twelve days leading up to Christmas Day.

PURPOSE

To bring joy to others during the Christmas season.

PREPARATION

Choose a friend or family for whom you'd like to perform this service. Familiarize yourself with the Christmas carol "The Twelve Days of Christmas," and think about small gifts that could represent the days mentioned. Purchase or gather the gifts and, during your family home evening, wrap the items and write accompanying explanatory notes. Decide what time of day is best to deliver the gifts to keep your identity anonymous. Start the delivery of this project on December 14 so that the twelfth day corresponds with Christmas Day.

POTENTIAL POSITIVE OUTCOMES

- A focus on giving during the Christmas season rather than receiving.
- Happiness that comes from giving service.

For I am desirous for the welfare of your souls. Yea, mine anxiety is great for you; and ye yourselves know that it has ever been.

—2 Nephi 6:3

22. REACH OUT

Contact a less active member of the Church.

PURPOSE

To give your brothers and sisters in the gospel an opportunity to return to the path toward salvation.

PREPARATION

Ask the full-time missionaries or ward mission leader to advise you about whom to visit and the best service you can render. Through prayer, select names of those who may be receptive to you. Decide upon the best approach to take, whether to make a telephone call, visit (by chance or appointment), or write a letter. Remember that a one-time contact will not be effective, so plan to continue your contacts over a period of time.

POTENTIAL POSITIVE OUTCOMES

- Restoration of a soul to the fold of God through development of friendships.
- An increased testimony of the importance of caring for the Lord's lost sheep.

Thou shalt open thine hand wide unto thy brother, to thy poor, and to thy needy, in thy land.

—Deuteronomy 15:11

23. TIME WISELY SPENT

Contact an organization and volunteer your time for one evening.

PURPOSE

To support those who are trying to make the world a better place.

PREPARATION

Select a charitable organization whose values and ethics are consistent with the teachings and standards of the Church. Contact them and explain that you are offering a few hours of service. Be flexible so that your volunteer time is convenient for all involved and help with whatever is most beneficial to the organization. You may like to make this a regular service opportunity.

POTENTIAL POSITIVE OUTCOMES

- Joy that comes from giving service.
- Assistance to those trying to make the world a better place in which to live.
- An increased testimony of the spiritual relationship that all mankind has as brothers and sisters.
- An ability to spread the message of Christ through your example of service.

Therefore, hold up your light that it may shine unto the world.

—3 Nephi 18:24

24. LIGHT OF THE WORLD

Spend your evening viewing Christmas lights.

PURPOSE

To help you feel the spirit of Christmas.

PREPARATION

Find out when and where Christmas light decorations will be displayed in your community. Local newspapers and radio stations often have this information available. Plan a route, either by car or on foot, to view the lights. You may invite others to join you or just relax and feel the Spirit on your own.

POTENTIAL POSITIVE OUTCOMES

- Reflection on the birth of the Savior and his role as the light of the world.
- Strengthened unity and love with those in your community.

And it came to pass that I, Nephi, did cause my people to be industrious, and labor with their hands.

—2 Nephi 5:17

25. GROW TOGETHER

Help a friend or neighbor with his gardening.

PURPOSE

To assist others in caring for and beautifying the Earth.

PREPARATION

A few weeks before this family home evening, contact a neighbor, ward member, friend, or relative and explain that you wish to help him work in his garden. Arrange a time and be willing to help with mowing, weeding, picking, digging, and planting. Offer to bring any gardening tools you own.

POTENTIAL POSITIVE OUTCOMES

- An increased testimony and appreciation for the creation of the world.
- Development of skills.
- Satisfaction from performing physical labor.

Rather then spend their days in idleness they would labor abundantly with their hands.

—Alma 24:18

26. A HELPING HAND

Help the ward activities committee prepare for an upcoming event.

PURPOSE

To fulfill your responsibility to sustain others in their callings.

PREPARATION

Be aware of upcoming ward activities. Contact your ward activities chairperson and explain that you would like to help as part of your personal family home evening program. Areas of assistance will vary depending on the activity but could include making decorations for a dance, delivering personal invitations to less-active members and investigators of the Church, or organizing some small part of the event.

POTENTIAL POSITIVE OUTCOMES

- Joy that comes from serving in the Church.
- Encouragement to others to magnify their callings.
- Nourishment of friendships with ward members as you work side by side.

And the bishop, also, shall receive his support, or a just remuneration for all his services in the church.

—Doctrine and Covenants 42:73

27. THANK YOU, BISHOP

Spend the evening washing the cars of your bishopric.

PURPOSE

To give an act of service to those who continuously serve you.

PREPARATION

Contact the members of the bishopric, including the executive secretary, and explain that you plan to visit each of their homes for family home evening to perform this act of service. You may wish to invite others to help you. Be prepared with buckets, sponges, and other car washing items necessary for the evening. If the bishopric members live long distances from each other, you may need to repeat this family home evening over a number of weeks.

POTENTIAL POSITIVE OUTCOMES

- Establishment of an example of service to the children of the bishopric.
- Encouragement to others to hold family home evening as you invite them to join you.
- Joy that comes from giving service.

The members should have the same care one for another. And whether one member should suffer, all the members suffer with it; or one member be honoured, all the members rejoice with it.

—1 Corinthians 12:25–26

28. A JOB WELL DONE

Express your joy for the achievement of another.

PURPOSE

To increase your ability to show genuine happiness for the accomplishments of others.

PREPARATION

Be aware of friends and family members who are reaching a goal or milestone in their lives. For example: a job promotion, graduation from high school or a university, the celebration of a wedding anniversary, the attainment of the Eagle Scout award, or other achievements. Decide how you would like to show your delight for their success. This could be as simple as a bunch of flowers, a card, or a letter. If you live close by, deliver your gift on the same family home evening night. If your chosen friend or family member lives far away, mail your gift the next day.

POTENTIAL POSITIVE OUTCOMES

- Overcoming jealousy.
- Nourishment of relationships as you encourage and praise others.

One Lord, one faith, one baptism, one God and Father of all, who is above all, and through all, and in you all.

—Ephesians 4:5–6

29. ON THE STRAIGHT AND NARROW

Prepare a small gift for someone who will shortly enter into the waters of baptism.

PURPOSE

To share your testimony of this sacred covenant.

PREPARATION

Become aware of children and adults in your ward who are preparing to be baptized. As you come to know them, purchase, make, or collect things that are appropriate to present as a baptismal gift such as a pocket-sized hymnal, a journal, some pictures of the Savior, or a collection of Church music. Include a letter containing your testimony. Prepare and wrap your items during your family home evening and, if appropriate, deliver your gift on the same night.

POTENTIAL POSITIVE OUTCOMES

- Remembrance of the feelings you had when you received baptism.
- Development of another's testimony of baptisms through your own.
- Fellowshipping of new members of the Church.

And are willing to bear one another's burdens, that they might be light; yea and are willing to mourn with those that mourn; yea and comfort those who stand in need of comfort.

—Mosiah 18:8–9

30. BEYOND THE VEIL

Write a letter of condolence to someone who has recently lost a friend or relative to death.

PURPOSE

To give others hope through your testimony of the Atonement of Jesus Christ.

PREPARATION

When writing your letter, be sensitive to the spiritual beliefs of those to whom you are writing. Make it a focus to pray for guidance during this family home evening and be worthy to receive promptings from the Holy Ghost. Have a pen, paper, envelope, your scriptures, appropriate postage, and the address of your friend or relative ready for use during the evening.

POTENTIAL POSITIVE OUTCOMES

- Comfort felt by those you love and care for.
- An increased testimony of eternal life and the Savior's role in making that possible.

For we are members one of another.

—Ephesians 4:25

31. UNITY

Get to know all the members of your ward a little better.

PURPOSE

To step outside of your comfort zone and make others feel welcome.

PREPARATION

Obtain an updated ward list from your ward clerk. Go through the list and identify the names of individuals and families with whom you are unfamiliar. Contact your ward mission leader or bishop to find out if any of these people should not be contacted. Once you have a final list, plan to introduce yourself to these members of your ward by writing a letter, making a scheduled visit, calling them on the telephone, or inviting them over for family home evening.

POTENTIAL POSITIVE OUTCOMES

- Commencement of new and eternal friendships.
- Increased confidence as you move outside your comfort zone.

Let every one of us please his neighbour for his good to edification.

—Romans 15:2

32. FHE PHANTOM

Deliver anonymous "knock-and-run" goodies to friends and family members in your neighborhood.

PURPOSE

To let others know that someone is thinking of them.

PREPARATION

Invite others to join you for this family home evening. You will need the use of a car, so if you don't own one, make sure you invite someone who does. Make a list of friends, relatives, and ward members who live in close proximity to one another and plan the route. On family home evening night, get together and make cookies or other treats to go into the goodie bags. Make sure you include a short message with each package to ensure the recipients know that it is specifically for them and from someone who knows and loves them. Have fun delivering the goodies to each home.

POTENTIAL POSITIVE OUTCOMES

- An occasion to show others how fun and rewarding family home evening can be.
- Joy that comes from giving service.
- Happiness felt by those who are on the receiving end of this activity.

And thou shalt have joy and gladness; and many shall rejoice at his birth.

—Luke 1:14

33. HAPPY BIRTHDAY

Send a birthday card to everyone you know who is having a birthday during a particular month.

PURPOSE

To let others know their birthdays are important to you.

PREPARATION

Identify the birthdays of friends and family members that will occur during the following month. Before your family home evening, organize cards (or supplies to make your own cards), pens, paper, envelopes, appropriate postage, and addresses. Spend your evening making and writing in the birthday cards. Address and stamp the envelopes, and mail them so they arrive close to the birthdays throughout the month.

POTENTIAL POSITIVE OUTCOMES

- Reflection on the purpose of birth in the Plan of Salvation.
- Appreciation and love felt by others on their special days.

What manner of communications are these that ye have one to another?

—Luke 24:17

34. COMMUNICATION

Make a long-distance or international telephone call to a friend or family member you have not spoken to in a long time.

PURPOSE

To maintain relationships over long distances and time.

PREPARATION

You may need to budget ahead for this family home evening. Contact your telephone company to find out the cheapest rates and times to call, and set a time limit if you have monetary restrictions. Call your friend or family member and enjoy your time together.

POTENTIAL POSITIVE OUTCOMES

- Renewal of friendships.

Cast me not off in the time of old age; forsake me not when my strength faileth.

—Psalm 71:9

35. ELDERLY CARE

Volunteer an evening of your time at an elderly care facility.

PURPOSE

To learn compassion for people of all ages.

PREPARATION

Identify an elderly care facility in your area. Contact the facility and explain that you would like to offer a few hours of volunteer work. Be prepared to assist the staff with any work they require, perhaps serving meals, sitting and talking with residents, or other activities. You may want to make this a regular part of your service to others.

POTENTIAL POSITIVE OUTCOMES

- Joy brought to those in their twilight years.
- Appreciation for your health and freedom your body has now.
- Creation of new friendships.

Only let your conversation be as it becometh the gospel of Christ: that whether I come and see you, or else be absent, I may hear of your affairs, that ye stand fast in one spirit, with one mind striving together for the faith of the gospel.

—Philippians 1:27

36. GREAT IDEA!

Invite friends over to brainstorm ideas for future family home evenings.

PURPOSE

To call upon the experiences and ideas of others to help one another hold meaningful and fun family home evenings.

PREPARATION

Talk with your single friends and arrange a time to hold family home evening that is convenient for everyone. Give music, prayer, and treat assignments. Have pens and paper ready to use on the night. In an atmosphere of love and fun, discuss the many options that are available for singles to create meaningful and enjoyable family home evenings. Encourage others to apply these ideas in their own lives as you do so in yours.

POTENTIAL POSITIVE OUTCOMES

- Discovery of new, inspirational, and fun family home evening ideas.
- Nourishment of friendships through sharing experiences and time together.
- An increased testimony of the importance of family home evening.

For I have learned by experience that the Lord hath blessed me for thy sake.

—Genesis 30:27

37. THE ROAD WELL TRAVELED

Visit with an elderly friend and engage in a meaningful conversation with them about their history.

PURPOSE

To learn, through the experience of an older generation, how to successfully walk the straight and narrow path back to our Heavenly Father.

PREPARATION

Select an elderly friend with whom you feel comfortable talking with. Arrange a time to have family home evening in his home at his convenience. If your friend is agreeable, you may wish to record your conversation. If so, make arrangements to bring a recording device with you. Have a list of questions prepared in advance to ask your friend to help prompt the memories and wisdom they have to share.

POTENTIAL POSITIVE OUTCOMES

- Direction and valuable advice given by those who have experienced much of life.
- Continuation of bonds and knowledge between generations.
- Assistance to others in having family home evening no matter what their stage of life.

To beautify the house of the LORD.

—Ezra 7:27

38. WORKING BEE

Spend some time helping care for your Sunday meeting-house.

PURPOSE

To increase your appreciation for the place in which you are able to worship the Savior every Sunday.

PREPARATION

Ask others to join you for this family home evening and contact person in charge of your building maintenance. Explain that you would like to do something extra to help care for the building as a family home evening service. Set a date and make arrangements to obtain keys and any equipment you may need. You may be asked to help with gardening, washing windows, dusting, cleaning bathrooms, mowing the lawn, or other jobs. Make sure you perform this service to the best of your ability.

POTENTIAL POSITIVE OUTCOMES

- Development of reverence for places where people gather to worship the Savior.

And healing every sickness and every disease among the people.

—Matthew 9:25

39. THE GIFT OF LIFE

Donate blood.

PURPOSE

To help others enjoy the same standard of health with which you are blessed.

PREPARATION

Confirm, with your doctor if necessary, that you are well enough to donate blood. Contact a reputable organization that receives blood donations and make an appointment. Ask any questions you may have if this is your first visit. Remember to eat before you go and rest after you donate blood. Asking one or two friends to join you for this family home evening may ease nervousness.

POTENTIAL POSITIVE OUTCOMES

- An increased testimony of the Word of Wisdom as you are able to donate clean and healthy blood.
- An ability for others to enjoy the benefits of a longer life with family and loved ones.
- Fears you may have are overcome.
- Gratitude for the medical and health services available to you.

And when thou art converted, strengthen thy brethren.

—Luke 22:32

40. ONWARD AND UPWARD

Have family home evening with someone you know is having a hard time.

PURPOSE

To help ease the burdens of another.

PREPARATION

Be mindful of friends or family members who may be struggling with an aspect of their life and invite them to join you for family home evening. Prayerfully ponder what kind of family home evening would be most helpful. With guidance from the Holy Ghost, be well prepared and make all the arrangements necessary to have a calm, fun, and spiritual evening.

POTENTIAL POSITIVE OUTCOMES

- Recognition of the love of the Savior during difficult times.
- Joy that comes from giving service.
- Nourishment of friendships.
- Encouragement for others to participate in family home evening.

And the land on the southward was called Bountiful, it being the wilderness which is filled with all manner of wild animals of every kind.

—Alma 22:31

41. ALL CREATURES OF OUR GOD AND KING

Visit a zoo or wildlife park in your area.

PURPOSE

To enjoy the creatures that God has created.

PREPARATION

Invite some friends to join you for this family home evening. Through the Internet, local tourist information center, or the telephone book, locate any animal parks, zoos, bird sanctuaries, farms, marine centers, and native wildlife sanctuaries in your area. Select a park and call for information such as entry fees, opening hours, and directions on how to get there.

POTENTIAL POSITIVE OUTCOMES

- Appreciation for the animals of the world.
- An awareness of the benefits of being close to nature.
- An increased respect for the creations of God.

And they did fellowship one with another, and did rejoice one with another, and did have great joy.

—Helaman 6:3

42. FUN AND GAMES

Invite friends over to play church games for the evening.

PURPOSE

To strengthen friendships and learn more about the gospel and each other.

PREPARATION

Explain your family home evening game night idea to a small number of your friends and use this opportunity to invite recent converts or less-active friends to join you. If you lack a supply of church games, borrow some from members of the ward or purchase them from a church bookstore or via the Internet. Make music, prayer, and treat assignments, and don't forget to follow up.

POTENTIAL POSITIVE OUTCOMES

- Encouragement for others to hold their own family home evenings.
- Development of eternal friendships.
- Fellowshipping in a nonthreatening environment for those in all stages of spiritual growth.

Let Israel rejoice in him that made him: let the children of Zion be joyful in their King. Let them praise his name in the dance: let them sing praises unto him with the timbrel and harp For the Lord taketh pleasure in his people.

—Psalm 149:2–4

43. DANCE PRACTICE

Spend your evening practicing new and appropriate dance steps.

PURPOSE

To engage in wholesome recreation.

PREPARATION

You have several options for this family home evening.

1. Rent or borrow an instructional video or DVD from your local library, rental store, friend, or family member. You'll have to secure a dancing partner or two for this evening and arrange with friends for a suitable time to have this family home evening.

2. Sign up for an introductory dance lesson. Look in your local newspaper, on bulletin boards, on the Internet, or in the telephone directory for places offering this kind of lesson.

3. You may know someone who is an accomplished dancer. Invite him, along with other friends, to join you for family home evening and teach you a few steps or routines. Make sure the time, venue, assignments, and any equipment needed are arranged conveniently for all involved.

POTENTIAL POSITIVE OUTCOMES

- Enjoyment of dancing while meeting standards set by the Lord.
- Development of skills and talents.
- Appreciation for the skills and talents with which others are blessed.

And also that every man should eat and drink, and enjoy the good of all his labour, it is the gift of God.

—Ecclesiastes 3:13

44. EAT, DRINK, AND BE MERRY

Prepare a picnic for a few friends.

PURPOSE

To enjoy good food and good company in good surroundings.

PREPARATION

Select a time of year suitable for outdoor dining for this activity. Invite a number of friends and family members on a picnic for family home evening. If your budget and time allow, prepare the entire picnic yourself. If not, make food, drink, utensil, and transportation assignments as well as those for music and prayer. Be sure to follow up on assignments given a few days before your scheduled family home evening. Have an alternative venue planned in case of bad weather.

POTENTIAL POSITIVE OUTCOMES

- Nourishment of friendships through spending relaxing and fun time together.
- Appreciation for the food and nature that is readily available to sustain and enrich your life.
- Motivation for others to have their own family home evenings.

He calleth together his friends and neighbours, saying unto them, Rejoice with me.

—Luke 15:6

45. PARTY TIME

Throw yourself a party.

PURPOSE

To celebrate an important event in your life with friends and family members.

PREPARATION

Choose an upcoming event that you would like to celebrate with others, perhaps your birthday, Christmas, graduation from school, or a national holiday. Spend a family home evening planning, preparing a budget, making invitations, and arranging food, music, games, a venue, decorations, and anything else you will need to celebrate. Remember, it's not so much the elaborate trimmings that people will remember but the fun and love they feel as they rejoice with you.

POTENTIAL POSITIVE OUTCOMES

- Further appreciation for an important event as you celebrate it with people you love.
- An opportunity to let others know they are important to you by including them in your special occasion.

Give instruction to a wise man, and he will be yet wiser: teach a just man, and he will increase in learning.

—Proverbs 9:9

46. TALENT NIGHT

Host a mini talent night.

PURPOSE

To appreciate others' unique gifts and talents.

PREPARATION

Decide upon a time and date for your family home evening and invite a number of friends and family members to join you. Ask them to prepare a small talent item to share with the group, such as telling an appropriate joke, playing a musical instrument, singing a song, reciting a poem, showing a completed craft, or performing a skit. You may even want to award fun prizes for the funniest talent, the loudest talent, the most innovative talent, and so forth. Be sure to share a talent of your own.

POTENTIAL POSITIVE OUTCOMES

- Development of friendships and self-confidence.
- Increased knowledge about your friends and family members.
- Motivation for others to have their own family home evenings.

And he shall turn the heart of the fathers to the children, and the heart of the children to the their fathers, lest I come and smite the earth with a curse.

—Malachi 4:6

47. FAMILY TIES

Make a video or DVD of your life for family members living far from you.

PURPOSE

To strengthen family ties.

PREPARATION

Choose the occasion for which you'd like to make the video or DVD. (Maybe just for fun). If you don't own recording equipment, rent or borrow some. Prepare an outline of your presentation in advance. Include shots of your neighbors, friends, the building where you work or go to school, and other people and places of interest where you live. Have packaging and a current address ready to send your video or DVD to your family immediately after your family home evening.

POTENTIAL POSITIVE OUTCOMES

- Creation of a record of you for future generations to enjoy.
- Nourishment of family relationships as you make efforts to keep in touch.

But we beseech you, brethren, that ye increase more and more; and that ye study to be quiet, and do your own business, and to work with your own hands.

—1 Thessalonians 4:10–11

48. A+

Make a study package for a friend.

PURPOSE

To help another reach his potential.

PREPARATION

Become aware of friends' exam timetables and select one or two to receive a study package. Before your family home evening purchase or collect items—pens, pencils, erasers, food, candy, chocolate, candles, and other fun stuff—for the package. Prepare a box and wrapping supplies. On the night of your family home evening, put the package together. You may like to include explanatory notes about each item. Deliver your package that night if possible.

POTENTIAL POSITIVE OUTCOMES

- Experiencing the joy of giving and helping.
- Appreciation for the hard work and sacrifices others make to achieve their goals.

And they sang together by course in praising and giving thanks unto the Lord.

—Ezra 3:11

49. HALLELUJAH

Host a hymn singing evening with friends and family members.

PURPOSE

To worship the Savior through song.

PREPARATION

You will need to enlist an accompanist, should you not be blessed with musical talent. You also need a venue that has a piano and enough room to hold all the people you invite. Ask everyone to bring a copy of *Hymns of The Church of Jesus Christ of Latter-day Saints*, and borrow a few extra copies from the ward library for those who forget. Make assignments for the treat and prayer before that evening. Spend your time singing the favorite hymns of those in attendance. Invite individuals to share stories about why particular hymns are special to them.

POTENTIAL POSITIVE OUTCOMES

- Strengthening of unity and testimony by praising the Savior with friends and family members.
- Development of friendships as you share sacred experiences with one another.
- Cultivation of singing talents.

For this is the message that ye heard from the beginning, that we should love one another.

—1 John 3:11

50. THE EXTRA MILE

Have family home evening with a family or individual you home or visit teach.

PURPOSE

To give extra support and friendship to whom you have been assigned to care.

PREPARATION

Arrange a date and time and, depending on space and convenience, hold the evening at your place or theirs. Organize hymns, prayers, a lesson, and treats that are suitable for all those involved. This is not to be counted as your visit for the month but rather an opportunity to stretch your hand of friendship

POTENTIAL POSITIVE OUTCOMES

- Positively influencing others to have family home evening.
- Satisfaction from dutifully and sincerely fulfilling important Church assignment.
- Enrichment of your own family home evening time by sharing it with others.
- Nourishment of friendship and testimonies.

Beloved, I wish above all things that thou mayest prosper and be in health.

—3 John 1:2

51. THE SIX BS

Organize a "B" sports evenings.

PURPOSE

To maintain your health through exercise.

PREPARATION

Decide on a "B" sport—badminton, basketball, bike riding, bungee jumping, baseball, or bowling—to enjoy. Invite the necessary number of friends and family members to join you. Organize a venue and gather the necessary sports equipment. Make any assignments in advance and don't forget to follow through. Play safely and courteously, showing good sportsmanship to others.

POTENTIAL POSITIVE OUTCOMES

- Maintenance of health and fitness.
- Enjoyment with the company of friends and family members.

Now my brethren, we see that God is mindful of every people, whatsoever land they may be in.

—Alma 26:37

52. INTERNATIONAL TIES

Invite someone who was born in another country to your home to share with you his culture.

PURPOSE

To expand your knowledge about your brothers and sisters living in different parts of the world.

PREPARATION

Select an international friend and decide which aspect of his culture you would like to learn about. Make any arrangement or purchases that will help your friend prepare more easily. For example, buy ingredients for any dishes they may wish to cook. Inviting a few friends from various nations can make your family home evening even more memorable.

POTENTIAL POSITIVE OUTCOMES

- Development of friendships.
- Increased knowledge about the world and its peoples.
- A desire to learn more about the lives of others.

Let us labor diligently; for if we should cease to labor, we should be brought under condemnation; for we have a labor to perform whilst in this tabernacle of clay.

—Moroni 9:6

Section 3: Temporal Focus

AN IDEA FOR EVERY WEEK OF THE YEAR

Every man shall be made accountable unto me, a steward over this own property.

—Doctrine and Covenants 42:32

1. BUDGET

Create, and resolve to live by a financial budget.

PURPOSE

To follow the counsel of President J. Ruben Clark who instructed us to "live within your means" (Conference Report, October 1937, 107).

PREPARATION

Obtain a copy of the *Marriage and Family Relations Participant Study Guide* from your ward library or Church distribution center. Make several copies of the budget form. You will also need paper, pens, bank account statements, receipts, bills, pay slips, and any other paperwork related to your income and expenses. Read through the "Managing Family Finances" chapter found on page 28 of the study guide. Fill out the budget form and make specific plans to follow the suggestions made in that chapter. President N. Eldon Tanner's talk, "Constancy Amid Change" from the October 1979 General Conference, is also recommended for frequent reading and inspiration regarding your finances.

POTENTIAL POSITIVE OUTCOMES

- Continuation down the road leading to debt-free life.
- Development of your testimony of the importance of paying tithes and offerings as the highest priority, whatever your financial situation.
- Improvement of your time management by having an easy and organized method by which to arrange your monetary obligations.

By much slothfulness the building decayeth; and through idleness of the hands the house droppeth through.

—Ecclesiastes 10:18

2. HOME REPAIRS

Find some things around your home that need fixing and fix them.

PURPOSE

To take care of the temporal goods that Heavenly Father has blessed you with.

PREPARATION

Go through your home and decide on a few projects that need your attention: the cupboard door that needs to be repaired, the burned-out light bulb that needs to be changed, the curtains that need to be washed and rehung, a loose door handle, or the wobbly table leg that needs to be fixed. Obtain any advice or instructions you need, and purchase the materials to fix those things you have chosen to repair or improve. Do not end your family home evening until all the projects are complete and the mess is cleaned up.

POTENTIAL POSITIVE OUTCOMES

- Improvement of home-maintenance skills.
- Appreciation for the temporal blessings you have.
- An awareness of the importance of your stewardship over those temporal blessings.
- Satisfaction from completion of tasks.

Thou shalt not idle away thy time, neither shalt thou bury thy talent that it may not be known.

—Doctrine and Covenants 60:13

3. NEW HOBBIES

Begin to cultivate a new interest.

PURPOSE

To improve your talents and expand your interests.

PREPARATION

Ponder the pastimes you've wanted to pursue but never had time or opportunity for, everything from aerobics to zoology. Choose a hobby that you can now begin and make any necessary preparations to start your new hobby on your family home evening night.

POTENTIAL POSITIVE OUTCOMES

- Discovery of a new talent.
- An increase of self-confidence.
- Productive use of time.

And they had appointed a man to be their king and leader over them.

—Alma 47:6

4. PATRIOTISM

Study the life of the current leader of your country.

PURPOSE

To expand your knowledge of your country's politics.

PREPARATION

From your local library or the Internet, gather information about the current leaders of your country. During your family home evening, read about their lives. Try to keep an open mind and suppress any previously conceived negative thoughts you've about these men and women.

POTENTIAL POSITIVE OUTCOMES

- Informative knowledge for the next time you are required to vote.
- Greater understanding as to why these leaders are the way they are, even if you would prefer someone else be in their positions.
- An ability to see these leaders as children of God.

Become acquainted with all good books, and with languages, tongues and people.

—Doctrine and Covenants 90:15

5. ANOTHER MAN'S SHOES

Read the biography of someone who has improved the lives of others through his or her efforts.

PURPOSE

To feel inspiration from those who live lives in the service of others.

PREPARATION

Make a list of people who have done extraordinary things for others with the talents that God has given them. From your local public library or friends, borrow a book about one of these people. Spend your family home evening reading this book.

POSITIVE POTENTIAL OUTCOMES

- A greater understanding about others' motivations and inspiration.
- Motivation to give service and improve your talents.

Till the ground, and raise all manner of grain and all manner of fruit of every kind.

—Mosiah 10:14

6. SOW A SEED

Plant any manner of vegetable, grain, herb, fruit, or flower that your circumstance allows.

PURPOSE

To follow the counsel of a prophet who said, "I hope we understand that, while having a garden, for instance, is often useful in reducing food costs and making available delicious fresh fruits and vegetables, it does much more than this" (Spencer W. Kimball, "And the Lord Called His People Zion," *Ensign*, August 1984, 5).

PREPARATION

Assess the possible area where you could grow and maintain a garden. Gather information about climate, water, soil requirements, and decide what to grow. Purchase or borrow the necessary gardening tools, equipment, seeds, and plants you will need. Spend the evening planting and organizing your garden, however small. Record in a permanent place the date, what you planted, and weather conditions to help improve your techniques from season to season.

POTENTIAL POSITIVE OUTCOMES

- Financial assistance through eating what you grow.
- An increase of self-sufficiency and skills.
- Appreciation for the creations of God.

And thus I did guard my people and my flocks, and keep them from falling into the hands of our enemies.

—Mosiah 10:2

7. SAFETY FIRST

Check all the areas in your home for physical safety.

PURPOSE

To be prepared for any physical danger that may occur.

PREPARATION

Make a list of areas you need to consider such as first-aid supplies, fire safety, burglary prevention, or storage of hazardous products. During your family home evening, go through your home, room by room, and scrupulously check all the danger areas you listed. Make notes about things you need to change, update, fix, or destroy. Set a reasonable date to finish your project. Start making the improvements that night and continue until the job is completed.

POTENTIAL POSITIVE OUTCOMES

- Peace every time you leave your home.
- Knowledge that you are fulfilling your stewardship over the temporal possessions you possess.
- Improvement of your physical environment.

Spin, and toil, and work, and work all manner of fine linen, yea and cloth of every kind, that we might clothe our nakedness.

—Mosiah 10:5

8. PATCHES

Spend the evening mending torn or worn out clothes.

PURPOSE

To implement the teaching of President Hinckley, "Our pioneer forebears lived by the adage, 'Fix it up, wear it out, make it do, or do without'" (Gordon B. Hinckley, "I Believe," *Ensign*, August 1992, 6).

PREPARATION

Gather together the clothes that need mending and purchase any notions and sewing materials you'll need to complete your tasks. If you need help with the project, invite a friend to teach you. Don't end your family home evening until everything is repaired. Even if you no longer wish to wear the clothes, they will be ready to donate to those who are in need.

POTENTIAL POSITIVE OUTCOMES

- Improvement of skills.
- Financial benefits through not having to purchase new clothes.
- An ability to focus on modest and respectable clothing rather than the fashion of the world.

Now it was the custom of the people of Nephi to call their lands. And their cities, and their villages, yea, even all their small villages, after the name of him who first possessed them.

—Alma 8:7

9. THE FOUNDING FATHERS

Research the name and settlement of the place where you live.

PURPOSE

To understand more about the locale in which you reside.

PREPARATION

Through the public library, Internet, or local, long-term residents in your neighborhood, gather information about the name and settlement of your town, city, state, or country. During your family home evening, study the information to increase your knowledge of the area where you live.

POTENTIAL POSITIVE OUTCOMES

- An increased knowledge about local history.
- Appreciation for the work of those who laid the foundations of your community.
- Gratitude for the opportunity to live where you do.
- A desire to be a better citizen.

And I God, made the beasts of the earth after their kind . . . and I God, saw that all these things were good.

—Moses 2:25

10. MAN'S BEST FRIEND

Take your neighbor's dog for a walk.

PURPOSE

To give service while improving your own physical health.

PREPARATION

Talk to your neighbors about this service and schedule a time to perform it. Plan the route you'll walk with the dog and the approximate time it will take, and let the owner know your findings. If you are unfamiliar with the dog, discuss any behavioral characteristics of which you need to be aware. Don't forget to take along the necessary gear to pick up deposits left by your charge.

POTENTIAL POSITIVE OUTCOMES

- Joy that comes from giving service.
- The formation of new friendships as you come into contact with dog owners.
- Improvement of physical health.
- Nourishment of friendships with the neighbors you serve.
- An appreciation for all God's creations.

But behold, this was an advantage to the Nephites . . . because of their much provision which they had laid up in store.

—3 Nephi 4:18

11. 72-HOUR PACK

Organize emergency supplies to last for a period of 72 hours.

PURPOSE

To be physically prepared should a disaster occur where you live.

PREPARATION

You may want to divide this night into two consecutive family home evenings, one for all the preparation and the other to put it all together. Obtain a list of needed items specifically designed for your local community and country. These can be found on the Internet, at local government offices, or from your ward emergency chairman. Edit the list to suit your personal circumstances. Purchase items that you don't have. Put your pack together and store it in an easily accessible place in your home. Set up a semiannual schedule to review and replace the supplies in your pack.

POTENTIAL POSITIVE OUTCOMES

- An increased chance of survival should an emergency occur.
- An ability to assist others in emergency situations.
- Peace that you are physically prepared for a crisis.

In the image of his own body, male and female, created he them, and blessed them.

—Moses 6:9

12. PHYSICAL HEALTH

Get a full medical examination from your doctor.

PURPOSE

To become aware of the physical condition of your body.

PREPARATION

If you do not have a regular doctor, now's a good time to find one. Ask friends or family members for recommendations. Make an appointment with your physician and take a list of questions concerning your health to your appointment. Record the results of the tests and your doctor's suggestions in a permanent file. Plan to repeat your check-up at least yearly.

POTENTIAL POSITIVE OUTCOMES

- An awareness of your physical condition.
- Maintenance of the temple of your spirit.
- An increased testimony of the marvelous creation of God that is your body.

Retire to thy bed early, that ye may not be weary; arise early, that your bodies and your minds may be invigorated.

—Doctrine and Covenants 88:124

13. RELAX!

Try a new relaxation technique.

PURPOSE

To understand the importance of relaxation and balance in your busy life.

PREPARATION

There are many new and different methods of relaxing that you can research in the public library, on the internet, or through friends, family members, and your doctor. Find one that appeals to you and obtain materials you'll need to completely enjoy this family home evening. If your chosen technique is successful in helping you feel calm and peaceful, plan to use it on a regular basis.

POTENTIAL POSITIVE OUTCOMES

- An opportunity to ponder quietly upon spiritual and temporal matters.
- The creation of balance in all areas of your life.

For verily, verily I say unto you, he that hath the spirit of contention is not of me, but is of the devil, who is the father of contention, and he stirreth up the hearts of men to contend with anger one with another.

—3 Nephi 11:29

14. ANGER MANAGEMENT

Release some built up tension and frustration.

PURPOSE

To appropriately deal with negative feelings you may have towards someone or something.

PREPARATION

This family home evening is for when you are not quite up to resolving anger issues face to face with other people. You'll need paper, a pen, and a box of matches. Simply write down all the negative feelings you have about a situation. Write exactly what you want to say, get everything off your chest. Once you are finished, read through what you have written a few times to make sure it's all there. Then, in a fireproof area, burn the papers, completely incinerating everything you wrote. The final and most important part of this family home evening is to then sincerely pray that you will be able to mend the scars left by the anger. You make want to end this night with a relaxation technique you found helpful during lesson thirteen—"Relax!"—in the Temporal Focus section.

POTENTIAL POSITIVE OUTCOMES

- An ability to put your feelings into perspective so you can work to resolve them.
- Expression of feelings without causing harm or

injury to another person, physically or emotionally.

- An increased testimony of the power of the Savior in helping you repent and improve in all areas of your life.
- A realization that solutions to problems can be found, rather than fueling them.

I, The Lord, stretched out the heavens, and built the earth, my very handiwork; and all the things therein are mine.

—Doctrine and Covenants 104:14

15. THE BEAUTY OF THE EARTH

Walk or drive to the top of a nearby hill and watch the sunrise or sunset.

PURPOSE

To more fully appreciate the creations of God.

PREPARATION

Decide upon a time (morning or night) and a place to have this family home evening. Check the seasonal times of the sunrise or sunset with your local weather bureau. Plan so that you have plenty of time to enjoy the scenery that will surround you as you enjoy this family home evening out-of-doors.

POTENTIAL POSITIVE OUTCOMES

- Increased testimony of Jesus Christ's role as creator.
- Quiet time to ponder upon spiritual and temporal matters.
- Improvement of your health through exercise and fresh air.

Yea, it shall come in a day when there shall be heard of fires, and tempests, and vapors of smoke in foreign lands; and there shall also be heard of rumors of wars and earthquakes in divers places. Yea, it shall come in a day when there shall be great pollutions upon the face of the earth; there shall be murders, and robbing, and lying, and deceiving, and whoredoms, and all manner of abominations.

—Mormon 8:29–31

16. PRACTICE MAKES PERFECT

Pretend there is a real emergency and use your 72-hour pack.

PURPOSE

To make sure you are prepared for a real emergency.

PREPARATION

This night should be held after lesson eleven, "72-Hour Pack," in the Temporal Focus section. Decide which emergency situation is most likely to occur in your neighborhood and act as though it has happened. Test out your emergency exits, food, sleeping gear, lighting, and heating devices. Don't forget to replenish anything that you use or change anything that doesn't suit your needs.

POTENTIAL POSITIVE OUTCOMES

- An appreciation for the comfort and safety in which you live at present.
- Improvement of your plans and resources for emergency preparedness.

That every man should bear rule in his own house.

—Esther 1:22

17. HOUSE RULES

Create some spiritual and temporal rules for your home.

PURPOSE

To have specific Christ-centered guidelines within which to live.

PREPARATION

All you'll need is paper and pens. Spend your evening writing down rules that you think are important to maintain a spiritual and safe environment in your home. Rules could include specific times to rise and sleep, minutes to spend studying the scriptures each day, forms of entertainment permitted, and appropriate Sabbath day activities. Refer to the Spiritual Focus section, lesson eleven, "Living in Righteousness" and lesson forty, "The Sabbath Day" for suggestions. Display these rules in a place easily observed by all who enter your home. Update and change your rules as necessary.

POTENTIAL POSITIVE OUTCOMES

- Expectations are known and therefore can be met by those who enter your home.
- A constant reminder of the standards you have set for yourself.

If thou art merry, praise the Lord with singing, with music.

—Doctrine and Covenants 136:28

18. ONE, TWO, THREE; ONE, TWO, THREE

Spend the evening learning how to direct hymns.

PURPOSE

To increase your musical talents.

PREPARATION

Obtain a copy of *Hymns of the Church of Jesus Christ of Latter-day Saints*. You'll also need the *Hymns* cassette tape or compact disc set and the *Music Training* video; both should be available from your ward library or can be purchased at a Church distribution center. Begin by viewing the video and then reading through the "For Beginning Music Directors" section of the hymn book found on pages 383–85. Select hymns that are familiar to you and, by following the video and the written directions, practice, practice, practice. Once you feel comfortable (this may take a number of family home evenings), contact your ward music chairperson and let him know you are available to lead congregational singing if needed.

POTENTIAL POSITIVE OUTCOMES

- An ability to assist others in fulfilling their callings.
- Increasing of your talents.
- Nourishment of your testimony through praising the Lord through music.

And they did not wear costly apparel, yet they were neat and comely.

—Alma 1:27

19. MODEST APPEARANCES

Go through your wardrobe and discard any clothing that does not meet the standards of the Church.

PURPOSE

To make daily decisions of what to wear always reflect the child of God that you are.

PREPARATION

Obtain a copy of *For the Strength of youth, Fulfilling Our Duty to God* pamphlet from your ward Young Men's or Young Women's president. Read pages 14–16, "Dress and Appearance," to get a clear understanding of what is required. Follow the advice at the end of page 16: "If you are not sure what is appropriate, ask your parents of leaders for help." The Holy Ghost will also guide you in deciding what is acceptable to the Lord and what is not. You can recycle unwanted clothes by using the material to make children's clothes, quilts, pillow cases and cushion covers, or by cutting them up for cleaning rags.

POTENTIAL POSITIVE OUTCOMES

- Consistency in feeling clean both inside and out.
- Assistance to those who have temporal needs to live more comfortably.
- Solidification of your commitment to keep temple covenants or preparing to do so.

Let him that is ignorant learn wisdom.

—Doctrine and Covenants 136:32

20. EVER LEARNING

Sign up for a free introductory class in something that interests you.

PURPOSE

To increase your skills and talents.

PREPARATION

Look in newspapers, in magazines, on television and on the Internet for advertisements offering free classes in various areas. Talking to friends and family members may also give you ideas of where classes may be offered. Once you find something that interests you, sign up for the class. You may like to invite someone to join you. If finances and interest allow, continue taking the class.

POTENTIAL POSITIVE OUTCOMES

- Establishment of new friendships
- Development of skills.
- Discovery of a new talent.

He considereth all their works.

—Psalm 33:15

21. ALL IN A DAY'S WORK

Update your curriculum vitae even if you are not intending to use it in the near future.

PURPOSE

To have this important document for use at any time.

PREPARATION

Find your old curriculum vitae. If you do not have access to a computer in your home, make arrangements to use a friend's or one at your local library during this family home evening. Read through your curriculum vitae and pencil in any changes or additions, and make these changes on the computer. Print off your new curriculum vitae and file it in a safe place for future use. You may like to make this a biannual family home evening to keep your curriculum vitae current.

POTENTIAL POSITIVE OUTCOMES

- Preparation should you need to use your curriculum vitae.
- A reminder of the accomplishments you have made.
- Gratitude for the opportunity to work.

Yes, all things which come of the earth, in the season thereof, are made for the benefit and the use of man.

—Doctrine and Covenants 59:18

22. THE CULINARY ARTS

Cook a seasonal recipe you have not yet tried.

PURPOSE

To learn to use seasonal produce in your cooking.

PREPARATION

Take a trip to the grocery store and make a list of all the foods that are in season, asking a store employee, if you are unsure. From your own recipe collection, a friend's or family member's, a collection on the Internet, or a cookbook at your local library, choose a recipe that you have not made before that uses the seasonal foods on your list. Purchase all that you will need and prepare it. You may like to invite someone to share it with you. If you like it, add it to your collection. If not, choose another recipe to try another time. You can also experiment by adapting a recipe with which you are already familiar by substituting current seasonal foods.

POTENTIAL POSITIVE OUTCOMES

- Expansion of your cooking repertoire.
- Knowledge of the creations of Heavenly Father and how they fit into the circle of life.

And I shall endeavor to write some of these things upon this record, for the benefit of my posterity that shall come after me.
—Abraham 1:31

23. FOR THEIR DAY

Make a time capsule.

PURPOSE

To preserve artifacts of your life for future generations to enjoy.

PREPARATION

Make a list of things to include in your time capsule. You might want to include your voice recorded on tape or video, current newspaper articles, the top-ten chart of your favorite music genre, a recording of your favorite television program, some photographs of things you do and use everyday, a catalogue showing the current prices of food and clothing, a copy of the Book of Mormon with your testimony written inside, and a copy of your family tree. Don't forget to include an explanatory note about each item you put in the time capsule. Obtain a container for your time capsule and decide where to keep it. Make a note of the location of your time capsule and when and by whom you'd like it opened. Keep this information with your other important documents.

POTENTIAL POSITIVE OUTCOMES

- Appreciation for the time in which you live.
- Creation of knowledge through which future generations can come to know you.

Be admonished: of making many books there is no end.

—Ecclesiastes 12:12

24. SHHHHH!

Visit your local public library.

PURPOSE

To discover the world of books.

PREPARATION

Locate your nearest public library and obtain a library card. Plan to spend a couple of hours browsing through the library on your family home evening. Familiarize yourself with all aspects of the library and don't hesitate to ask questions. Check out a number of books that interest you to take home to read.

POTENTIAL POSITIVE OUTCOMES

- Expansion of learning opportunities.
- Enjoyment that comes from good books at little or no cost.

Therefore, brethren, stand fast, and hold to the traditions which ye have been taught.

—2 Thessalonians 2:15

25. TRADITIONS

Create a permanent listing of your traditions.

PURPOSE

To possess a resource of your personal traditions.

PREPARATION

Think about holidays, birthdays, and other times when you traditionally do something. Gather photo albums and scrapbooks to look through during your family home evening. As you browse through the photographs, write down all the traditions that you recall. Include the occasion, those who are usually present, specific details relevant to each event, and why the tradition is important to you. Also list other traditions you would like to start in the future. Once you have a rough draft, type it on a computer. Make your collection into a booklet or keep it in a folder. Frequently review it, and continue to add traditions as you go throughout the year.

POTENTIAL POSITIVE OUTCOMES

- Recollection of good memories.
- Appreciation for those who started these traditions in your life.
- A renewal of good traditions in your life.

Therefore shall ye observe this day in your generations . . . forever.

—Exodus 12:17

26. HAPPY HOLIDAYS

Learn the history behind an upcoming holiday and make some traditional decorations for your home.

PURPOSE

To know the true meaning behind celebrations in your country.

PREPARATION

Choose an upcoming holiday and learn the history behind this celebration. During your study, find out about traditional decorations, food, and customs related to this holiday. Select a few that you would like to incorporate into your celebration this year. Make any purchases or borrow anything you will need before your family home evening. Spend your evening making decorations and food in readiness for the occasion.

POTENTIAL POSITIVE OUTCOMES

- A deeper understanding about celebrations in your country.
- Enjoyment as you make this celebration more meaningful and personal.

And they did work all manner of work of exceeding curious workmanship.

—Ether 10:27

27. IN THE EYE OF THE BEHOLDER

Visit a museum.

PURPOSE

To enjoy the beauty of art.

PREPARATION

Locate museums and art galleries in your area, looking for exhibitions that may interest you. Check the hours and entry fees. Try to visit during your normally scheduled family home evening time.

POTENTIAL POSITIVE OUTCOMES

- An awareness of opportunities to enjoy art in your community.
- Appreciation for the skills and talents of others.

For the Lord God giveth light unto the understanding; for he speaketh unto men according to their language, unto their understanding.

—2 Nephi 31:3

28. HELLO, KONNICHIWA, BONJOUR

Begin the study of a new language.

PURPOSE

To bring you closer to your brothers and sisters throughout the world.

PREPARATION

There are numerous ways to study a language, including studying with a native speaker, listening to tapes, watching television programs and videos, using textbooks and dictionaries, learning on the Internet, and enrolling in a class. After investigating the resources available in your community for the language of your choice, select the method best suited to your time and financial needs. Make all the arrangements you need to incorporate this into your family home evening. One night of study may be enough for you, or you may want to continue studying on a regular basis.

POTENTIAL POSITIVE OUTCOMES

- Interaction with and learning about people from different cultures other than your own.
- An increase of your skills and talents.
- Confidence in your abilities.
- Opportunities for travel, work, and friendships.
- Unity with people of all nations.

And now I, Mormon, make a record of the things which I have both seen and heard.

—Mormon 1:1

29. ALL ABOUT ME

Write a brief personal history.

PURPOSE

"Be a record-keeping people" (Spencer W. Kimball, "President Kimball Speaks Out on Personal Journals," *Ensign,* December 1980, 61).

PREPARATION

Decide if you are going to keep your record on computer, in a journal, or in a folder. Make sure you have all the appropriate things you'll need, and also have photographs, old journals, letters, and memorabilia to help remind you of past events. Keep it simple. Begin by creating a time line, using the years of your life. Write a few lines about each year, highlighting major milestones. If you enjoy writing, expand your record with experiences and stories. Don't consider this family home evening finished until you bring events up to date to the present year. Make a goal to update this personal history annually.

POTENTIAL POSITIVE OUTCOMES

- Enjoyment from reminiscing over past experiences in your life.
- Qualification for blessings that come from following prophetic counsel.
- Creation of an influential record for your posterity.

Even so I would that ye should remember.

—Mosiah 4:11

30. LEST WE FORGET

Visit a memorial in your city.

PURPOSE

To remember those who have lived before.

PREPARATION

If you are not familiar with memorial sites in your area, call your city office or tourist bureau for information. Some memorials may have restricted visiting hours, so schedule this family home evening accordingly. Choose the number of memorials you can visit on the same evening. Take your time. Read all the information and names written around the memorials. Try to learn why these memorials have been erected. This can be a very touching and spiritual experience.

POTENTIAL POSITIVE OUTCOMES

- Knowledge of people in the area in which you live.
- Appreciation for the sacrifice and feeling the spirit of those who have lived before.
- The desire to make the world a better place.
- Realization that one person can make a difference.

Whatsoever thy hand findeth to do, do it with thy might.

—Ecclesiastes 9:10

31. MR. FIX-IT

Learn some simple bicycle or car repairs skills.

PURPOSE

To increase your self-sufficiency.

PREPARATION

If you don't own a bicycle or car, invite a friend or family member to join you. Decide beforehand what you'd like to learn. If you already know how to change a flat tire, choose something a little more challenging. Through the resources of your local library, the Internet, friends, and family members in the know, gather instructions and find out what materials you will need. Be patient and careful, and remember that you don't need to be perfect the first time you try something new. This is a learning exercise, and practice will help you master the skill you've chosen to learn for this family home evening.

POTENTIAL POSITIVE OUTCOMES

- Development of self-confidence and skills.
- Satisfaction that comes from accomplishing a task.
- An ability to help others in need should they encounter the problem you have been able to fix.

Are thou in health, my brother?

—2 Samuel 20:9

32. STEP BY STEP

Take a long walk.

PURPOSE

To increase your physical fitness.

PREPARATION

If you are physically able, walk for at least an hour. Plan out a route either mentally or on a map. Make sure that you have appropriate shoes and clothing for exercise. If you feel unsafe walking alone, invite someone to join you.

POTENTIAL POSITIVE OUTCOMES

- Commencement of a good exercise habit.
- An increased knowledge and testimony that your body is a temple that houses your spirit.
- Enjoyment of the creations of God around you as you walk among them.

Behold, I have given unto you the names of our first parents who came out of the land of Jerusalem; and this I have done that when you remember your names ye may remember them; and when ye remember them ye may remember their works; and when ye remember their remember their works ye may know how it is said, and also written, that they were good.

—Helaman 5:6

33. MY NAME IS . . .

Research the meaning of your name.

PURPOSE

To understand more about who you are.

PREPARATION

If you don't already know, ask your parents why they chose your name. Using baby-name books or the Internet, research what your name means, collecting information such as the country or language of origin, other names with similar meanings, and the spelling and attributes associated with your name. Write this information in your journal or add it to your personal and family history information. If you have been given a relative's name, search for information about their life. A study of the *Topical Guide* under the entry "Name" is a great addition to this family home evening.

POTENTIAL POSITIVE OUTCOMES

- Realization of the importance of names.
- Formation of closer relationships to relatives as you study their names.

The flowers appear on earth; the time of the singing of birds is come.

—Song of Solomon 2:12

34. NATIONAL PRIDE

Study about the national emblems of your country.

PURPOSE

To learn more about the land of your inheritance.

PREPARATION

National emblems include birds, flowers, animals, flags, and other objects. From resources such as tourist information centers, your government office, the Internet and public library, gather and sort through this information, collecting pieces that are of particular interest to you. Store this information for future reference.

POTENTIAL POSITIVE OUTCOMES

- An increase of national pride.
- Greater respect for things associated with the history of your country.

But if ye are prepared ye shall not fear.

—Doctrine and Covenants 38:30

35. BE PREPARED

Gather all the important documents for emergency evacuation purposes.

PURPOSE

To be prepared in case of an emergency.

PREPARATION

Locate all of your important documents, such as your birth certificate, driver's license, bank cards, university graduation certificate, insurance documents, temple recommend, and four-generation family group sheet. Make copies of these documents and have them signed and dated by yourself and two witnesses. Laminate them or store them in watertight plastic bags or containers. Keep your documents in a secure area of your home that is easily accessible should an emergency such as a fire or flood occur. Update them on a regular basis as you come into possession of new, important documents or when existing ones become outdated.

POTENTIAL POSITIVE OUTCOMES

- Peace of mind concerning this aspect of your life.
- The ability to sort out problems smoothly through this preparation should the need arise.

Such as healing the sick, raising the dead, causing the lame to walk, the blind to receive their sight, and the deaf to hear, and curing all manner of diseases.

—Mosiah 3:5

36. AN APPLE A DAY

Organize all your home medicinal needs.

PURPOSE

To care for the body with which God has blessed you.

PREPARATION

This family home evening is to ensure that you have an up-to-date medicine cabinet and/or first aid kit in your home. Make a list of all the medicinal supplies and prescriptions you regularly use. Add others that you may need in an emergency. Purchase the items you do not have and replace any that are out of date. Make sure that the place where you keep all of your medical supplies is lockable or out of the reach of children, even if you don't have any. Regularly check your supplies and update them as necessary.

POTENTIAL POSITIVE OUTCOMES

- Healthier living.
- Self-sufficiency and organization to care for minor ailments at home.

And the earth brought firth grass, and herb yielding seed after his kind, and the tree yielding fruit, whose seed was in itself, after his kind: and God saw that it was good.

—Genesis 1:12

37. NEVER HUNGER

Learn how to preserve fruit and vegetables.

PURPOSE

To be able to include fruits and vegetables as part of your twelve month supply of food storage.

PREPARATION

Decide which foods you are going to preserve, and which method of preservation best suits your circumstances. The Internet, a public library, and your Relief Society president are good sources of information. Food preservation methods include drying, bottling, stewing, and jamming. Plan to use fruits and vegetables that are in season since they are usually cheaper. Spend the evening preserving the food of your choice. You may like to combine this family home evening with lesson thirteen, "Harvest Season," in the Social Focus section, and lesson forty-four, "One Year's Supply" in the Temporal Focus section.

POTENTIAL POSITIVE OUTCOMES

- Development of a new skill
- Preparation of extra food to eat in an emergency.

In a dream, in a vision of the night, when deep sleep falleth on men, in slumberings upon the bed; then he openeth the ears of men, and sealeth their instruction.

—Job 33:15–16

38. GOOD NIGHT

Start a dream journal.

PURPOSE

To record significant dreams.

PREPARATION

Obtain a notebook and a pen to record your dreams. During your family home evening, ponder the dreams you've had that remain vivid to this day. Record what you can remember of these dreams, including the date and the place where you had the dream. Keep this notebook near where you usually sleep so you can continually record dreams that you feel are significant.

POTENTIAL POSITIVE OUTCOMES

- Recognition and remembrance of messages that come from the heavens.

And gave unto him a book, and bade him that he should read.

—1 Nephi 1:11

39. ONCE UPON A TIME

Start reading a classic book of literature.

PURPOSE

To value great works of writing.

PREPARATION

Talk with a friend or family member who likes to read and whose opinion you trust. Ask him to suggest a book that may be of interest to you. Buy the book or borrow it from your local library. Spend the evening relaxing and reading. When you've finished the book, if you enjoyed it, recommend it to someone else.

POTENTIAL POSITIVE OUTCOMES

- Expansion of your imagination and opening of a whole new world of learning opportunities.
- Appreciation for the talents of those who have the gift to write.
- Pleasure and value from reading as a form of entertainment.
- An ability to share with others what you have enjoyed.

Yea, for they did visit many parts of the land.

—Helaman 11:33

40. LOCAL EXPLORATION

Visit local places of historic and sightseeing interest.

PURPOSE

To learn more about the area in which you live.

PREPARATION

Pay a visit to your local tourist information center and collect information on places that interest you. Choose a place to visit and make the necessary arrangements. You may like to spend a series of family home evening visiting places in your area. Other family home evening ideas that will compliment this one are lesson twenty-seven, "In the Eye of the Beholder" and lesson thirty, "Lest we Forget," both in the Temporal Focus section.

POTENTIAL POSITIVE OUTCOMES

- Appreciation for the area in which you live.
- An increased knowledge about the place where you live.

And now I know that this love which thou hast had for the hildren of men is charity.

—Ether 12:34

41. RECYCLED FUN

Donate old toys and games to children in need.

PURPOSE

To bring happiness to children in your community.

PREPARATION

Go through your closets and pull out old games and toys that you have not used within the last year. Fix those that need a little repair and throw out the broken items. Donate your toys and games to hospitals, orphanages, your ward nursery, childcare centers, or schools. Contact the place and make arrangements to deliver them, or arrange to have them collected from your home.

POTENTIAL POSITIVE OUTCOMES

- An opportunity to give to others enjoyment.
- Joy that comes giving service.
- Gratitude for the temporal possessions you have been blessed with.

And let ours also learn to maintain good works for the necessary uses, that they be not unfruitful.

—Titus 3:14

42. CHECKLIST

Plan your week and accomplish as many errands as you can in one night.

PURPOSE

To overcome procrastination.

PREPARATION

All you'll need to begin is your calendar or planner, a pen, and a piece of paper. Sit down and plan out the week ahead. Write down everything you need and want to do during the next seven days. Review the list and choose those things that you can do that night and do them. Some may involve leaving your home, while others can be done around the house. Do not finish your family home evening until you have completed everything you wrote on your second list.

POTENTIAL POSITIVE OUTCOMES

- Easement of stress by completing numerous tasks at one time.
- A resolution to stop procrastinating.
- Freedom that comes from being organized.

And God called the dry land earth; and the gathering together of the waters called he Seas: and God saw that it was good.

—Genesis 1:10

43. WET 'N WILD

Spend some time in the water.

PURPOSE

To make use of community and natural water facilities available to you.

PREPARATION

If you have a fear of water, you can spend this family home evening relaxing in the bath or running under the sprinkler. For the rest, decide whether you want to enjoy the water at your local community pool, in the ocean or a lake, water skiing, fishing, snorkeling, diving, or spending time at a spa or hot spring. If you are planning to enjoy this family home evening alone, be sure to tell someone trustworthy where you are going and when you plan to return home. Check in with this person when you arrive home.

POTENTIAL POSITIVE OUTCOMES

- Increased physical fitness through an activity that you enjoy.
- Gratitude for opportunities that are available to you.

That every man who has need may be amply supplied ad receive according to his wants.

—Doctrine and Covenants 42:33

44. ONE YEAR'S SUPPLY

Begin a goal to have one year's supply of food storage.

PURPOSE

To be self-sufficient in times of need.

PREPARATION

Talk to your ward welfare specialist, Relief Society president, or elders quorum president. Explain that you are preparing to store food and that you need their advice. Have a list of question ready to ask when you meet with them. On the night of family home evening, draw up your final plan for food storage. This will include where and how to store your food, what you will store, your financial commitments to storing food, and how you will turn over your storage. Clear out a storage area and start transferring some food.

POTENTIAL POSITIVE OUTCOMES

- Preparation for an emergency.
- Development of your budgeting and planning skills.

And the Gods saw that they would be obeyed, and that their plan was good.

—Abraham 4:21

45. FHE

Plan your family home evenings for the next couple of months.

PURPOSE

To successfully hold family home evening every week.

PREPARATION

You will need a copy of this book, other resources with family home evening ideas, your calendar, and a place to record your plans. Select the specific date each week to have family home evening and mark it on your calendar or in your diary, listing your proposed activity for the night. Also list what you will need to do to prepare for each family home evening. Make this planning night a monthly, quarterly, or biannual activity.

POTENTIAL POSITIVE OUTCOMES

- Preparation and readiness for family home evening each week.
- An ability to keep family home evening as a top priority in your life.
- Development of organization skills.

And that ye may put difference between holy and unholy, and between unclean and clean.

—Leviticus 10:10

46. SPRING CLEANING

Clean your home from top to bottom.

PURPOSE

To have a physically clean home where the Spirit can dwell.

PREPARATION

Gather together all your cleaning equipment, checking to see if you need to purchase any new cleaning products. Do a general tidy up, and then start cleaning room by room. Be sure to vacuum, sweep, wax, dust, air out, wash, rinse, polish, wipe, and scrub everything in sight.

POTENTIAL POSITIVE OUTCOMES

- Satisfaction as you complete a major task.
- Creation of a clean atmosphere where the Spirit can dwell.
- Initiation of good hygiene habits.

Thou shalt live together in love, insomuch that thou shalt weep for the loss of them that die.

—Doctrine and Covenants 42:45

47. RESPECT FOR THE DEAD

Visit the grave of someone you know.

PURPOSE

To recapture fond memories forged by association with those who have moved beyond the veil.

PREPARATION

Check to see if the cemetery or burial place has restricted visiting hours and also the condition of the burial site. Take any equipment you might need for weeding, picking up litter, and polishing. Place a picture of the deceased person in a clearly visible spot in your home or at work for the week leading up to your visit. This will help to prompt memories and keep you aware of the importance of this family home evening. Remember to take flowers, or some other token traditional in your country, to show respect and love for the departed. If there are other graves nearby that look neglected, spend some time beautifying them also.

POTENTIAL POSITIVE OUTCOMES

- Recollection of pleasant memories.
- An increased testimony of the life after our mortal probation.
- Preservation of sacred sites.

Therefore, choose you by the voice of this people, judges, that ye may be judges according to the laws which have been given you by our father, which are correct, and which were given them by the hand of the Lord.

—Mosiah 29:25

48. THE POWER OF CHOICE

Study about candidates for an upcoming political election.

PURPOSE

To exercise your power of the vote to benefit you and your fellow men.

PREPARATION

Make sure that you are registered to vote, and be aware of upcoming elections. Gather information about all the candidates by contacting political party offices, using the Internet, and reading information dropped in your mailbox. During your family home evening, study the information, making notes along the way. Once you have made a decision about your voting preferences, pray to ask Heavenly Father for confirmation that these are the people he would like to have speaking on behalf of your community.

POTENTIAL POSITIVE OUTCOMES

- An awareness of the importance of your vote.
- Support of community leaders who are following the teachings of Christ.
- Appreciation for your freedom of choice.

Yea, it had a more powerful effect upon the minds of the people than the sword, or anything else, which had happened to them.

—Alma 31:5

49. MEDIA WATCH

Write a letter of praise or concern to a media company that has influenced you.

PURPOSE

To promote community entertainment that is in keeping with the teachings of the Savior.

PREPARATION

Spend a few weeks before this family home evening really concentrating on the standard of television, magazines, and radio programs available, noting how they affect you. Make notes of dates, times, and names of broadcast details or publication information. Gather the relevant contact addresses for the company to which you choose to write. In your letter express your feelings in a Christlike manner, and offer suggestions for improvement. You may wish to make this a regular event as you witness the decline of censorship standards in your community.

POTENTIAL POSITIVE OUTCOMES

- Encouragement to those that produce wholesome entertainment to continue to do so.
- Discouragement to those that produce unwholesome entertainment to stop doing so.
- Solidification of your personal viewing, listening, and reading standards to conform to the teachings of Jesus Christ.

And Jesus went about all Galilee . . . healing all manner of sickness and all manner of disease among the people.

—Matthew 4:23

50. FIRST AID

Learn some basic first aid skills.

PURPOSE

To increase your ability to care for your body.

PREPARATION

There are a number of options for this family home evening. You may want to invite someone you know who is a registered nurse, midwife, doctor, or other medical professional to your home to share some of his skills. Alternatively, you can enroll in a first-aid course. A third option is to borrow books, videos, or DVDs related to this subject from your local library and spend the evening studying them. As part of your family home evening, make a list of extra medical supplies you need to add to your first-aid kit. See lesson thirty-six, "An Apple A Day," in the Temporal Focus section for more information.

POTENTIAL POSITIVE OUTCOMES

- Increased knowledge about the human body.
- Development of new skills.
- An ability to help others and yourself in times of minor medical emergencies.

And God said, Let the earth bring forth the living creature after his kind, and creeping thing, and beast of the earth after his kind. And so God made the beast of the earth after his kind, and cattle after their kind, and everything that creepeth upon the earth after his kind: and God saw that it was good.

—Genesis 1:24–25

51. ALL CREATURES OF OUR GOD AND KING

Volunteer some time at an animal shelter.

PURPOSE

To increase your respect for the creations of God.

PREPARATION

Through the Internet or local telephone directory find organizations that care for lost, abandoned, and sick animals in your community. Contact them, explaining your desire to volunteer a few hours of service, and make the necessary arrangements. You may wish to continue doing this service on a regular basis.

POTENTIAL POSITIVE OUTCOMES

- Assistance to others who are working to improve the lives of animals.
- An awareness of the responsibility and stewardship you have for all creatures that dwell on the Earth.

Now, there is a death which is called a temporal death.

—Alma 11:42

52. JUST IN CASE

Write out your funeral or memorial service wishes.

PURPOSE

To ease the burden of loved ones when you are called to the other side of the veil.

PREPARATION

Ponder on people and music that have special meaning to you. Write down the hymns and songs you wish to have sung, those you want to be invited to speak, a venue, and anything else that needs to happen at your funeral. Also, include things you do not want done. Date and sign your list. Keep this in a secure place and make necessary changes as your circumstances and preferences change. Also, make a copy for your family or bishop to keep on file.

POTENTIAL POSITIVE OUTCOMES

- Peace as you know your wishes are expressed.
- Assistance to loved ones should you suddenly depart this life.
- Nourishment of your testimony of eternal life.

List of Focus Topics

Spiritual Focus

1. Just for You 24
2. Mission in Life 26
3. Q & A......................... 27
4. Temple Worship.......... 28
5. Sing, Sing a Song........ 30
6. Scripture Heroes......... 31
7. Family History? Help!........................... 32
8. Gratitude 33
9. Listen.......................... 34
10. Anytime, Anywhere, Anyplace 35
11. Living in Righteousness 36
12. A Record for Posterity...................... 38
13. Sunday School Study........................... 40
14. A Name and a Blessing....................... 41
15. Two Short Years.......... 42
16. Easter.......................... 43
17. Proclaim the Gospel......................... 44
18. Priesthood or Relief Society Study 45
19. Journal Entries............ 46
20. Mission Music 48
21. Church Literature....... 49
22. The True Meaning of Christmas.................... 50
23. Share Your Experiences................. 51
24. The Sacramental Prayers......................... 52
25. Video Night................ 53
26. Goals........................... 54
27. Even the Little Things 55
28. The Law of the Fast 56
29. Called to Serve............ 57
30. Message of Love 58
31. Sacrifice....................... 59
32. Future Leaders............ 60
33. Perfection.................... 61
34. Service in the Kingdom of God......................... 62
35. One Hundred Percent...63
36. For Our Time 64
37. General Conference.... 65
38. The Twelve Tribes of Israel............................ 66
39. Four Generations........ 67
40. The Sabbath Day......... 69
41. A Sacred Record......... 70
42. Count Your Blessings...71
43. Servants of the Lord............................ 72
44. Sacred Music 73
45. A Daily Reminder 74
46. Successful Endurance................... 75
47. Preparing for Eternity....................... 77
48. The Holy Priesthood of God............................. 79
49. Psalms and Proverbs 81
50. Family Home Evening Folder.......................... 82
51. A Covenant People..... 84
52. We Believe.................. 85

Social Focus

1. Welcome..................... 88
2. Citizens of Example...................... 89
3. Mother's Day.............. 90
4. Honesty is the Best Policy 91
5. The Welfare of Others......................... 92
6. Charitable Donations ...93

7. Bear No Malice........... 94
8. Serve Thy Master........ 95
9. Long Lost Friends...... 96
10. Make Yourself at Home.......................... 97
11. Surprise!...................... 98
12. Father's Day................ 99
13. Harvest Season..........100
14. Keeping in Touch.......101
15. Warm Food and a Warm Heart..........................102
16. Congratulations.........103
17. The Sick and the Needy.........................104
18. A Pleasing Environment..............105
19. Blessed Be His Name.........................106
20. Date Night.................107
21. Twelve Days of Christmas..................108
22. Reach Out.................109
23. Time Wisely Spent....110
24. Light of the World.....111
25. Grow Together...........112
26. A Helping Hand........113
27. Thank You, Bishop.....114
28. A Job Well Done.......115
29. On the Straight and Narrow......................116
30. Beyond the Veil..........117
31. Unity.........................118
32. FHE Phantom...........119
33. Happy Birthday.........120
34. Communication.........121
35. Elderly Care..............122
36. Great Idea!.................123
37. The Road Well Traveled.....................124
38. Working Bee.............125
39. The Gift of Life..........126
40. Onward and Upward......................127
41. All Creatures of Our God and King............128
42. Fun and Games..........129
43. Dance Practice...........130
44. Eat, Drink, and Be Merry.........................132
45. Party Time.................133
46. Talent Night..............134
47. Family Ties...............135
48. A+.............................136
49. Hallelujah.................137
50. The Extra Mile..........138
51. The Six Bs.................139
52. International Ties......140

Temporal Focus

1. Budget.........................142
2. Home Repairs.............143
3. New Hobbies..............144
4. Patriotism....................145
5. Another Man's Shoes...146
6. Sow a Seed..................147
7. Safety First..................148
8. Patches........................149
9. The Founding Fathers...150
10. Man's Best Friend......151
11. 72-Hour Pack............152
12. Physical Health..........153
13. Relax!.........................154
14. Anger Management...155
15. The Beauty of the Earth.........................157
16. Practice Makes Perfect........................158
17. House Rules..............159
18. One, Two, Three; One, Two, Three..................160
19. Modest Appearances...161
20. Ever Learning............162
21. All in a Day's Work....163
22. The Culinary Arts......164
23. For Their Day............165
24. Shhhhh!.....................166
25. Traditions...................167
26. Happy Holidays.........168
27. In the Eye of the Beholder....................169
28. Hello, Konnichiwa, Bonjour......................170
29. All about Me.............171
30. Lest We Forget..........172
31. Mr. Fix-it.................173
32. Step by Step..............174
33. My Name Is 175
34. National Pride...........176
35. Be Prepared...............177
36. An Apple a Day.........178
37. Never Hunger............179
38. Goodnight.................180
39. Once upon a Time.....181
40. Local Exploration......182
41. Recycled Fun............183
42. Checklist....................184
43. Wet 'n Wild..............185
44. One Year's Supply......186
45. FHE..........................187
46. Spring Cleaning.........188
47. Respect for the Dead..........................189
48. The Power of Choice...190
49. Media Watch............191
50. First Aid....................192
51. All Creatures of Our God and King............193
52. Just in Case...............194

Sources

Andersen, Neil A. "Prophets and Spiritual Mole Crickets," *Ensign*, November 1999, 17.

Ashton, Marvin J. "Straightway," *Ensign*, May 1983, 32.

Christensen, Val R. "Overcoming Discouragement," *Ensign*, November 1998, 31.

Clark, J. Reuben. In Conference Report, October 1937, 107.

Dew, Sheri L. "Are We Not All Mothers?" *Ensign*, November 2001, 96.

Eyring, Henry B. "Do Not Delay," *Ensign*, November 1999, 33.

Faust, James E. "Enriching Our Lives through Family Home Evening," *Ensign*, June 2003, 3.

"First Presidency Preface," *Hymns* [1985], x.

Haight, David B. "A Foundation Whereon Men Cannot Fall," *Ensign*, July 1972, 107.

Hinckley, Gordon B. "I Believe," *Ensign*, August 1992, 6.

———. "News of the Church," *Ensign*, April 1996, 74.

Kimball, Spencer W. "And the Lord Called His People Zion," *Ensign*, August 1984, 5.

———. "Let Us Move Forward and Upward," *Ensign*, May 1979, 84.

———. "President Kimball Speaks Out on Personal Journals," *Ensign*, December 1980, 61.

———. "The True Way of Life and Salvation," *Ensign*, May 1978, 4.

Komatsu, Adney Y. "The Blessing of Building a Temple," *Ensign*, May 1976, 101.

Romney, Marion G. "News of the Church," *Ensign*, September 1973, 83.

Smoot, Mary Ellen. "Family History: A Work of Love," *Ensign*, March 1999, 15.

Wirthlin, Joseph B. "Spiritually Strong Homes and Families," *Ensign*, May 1993, 69.

About the Author

Tamara Leigh Woolley was born on the island state of Tasmania, Australia, where she graduated from university with Japanese and education degrees. She was baptized a member of The Church of Jesus Christ of Latter-day Saints at age eight. Now, as a thirteen-year veteran of the Church's young single adult program, Tamara has held stake leadership positions in this area for many years. During this time, she has developed an appreciation for family home evening among single members of the Church.

Tamara served a mission to Kobe, Japan, from 1996-1998 and fell in love with the country and its people. She now lives and works in Tokyo, Japan at the American School in Japan where she teaches kindergarten.

Tamara loves to swim, watch the Australian sport of cricket, and research family history. She also cannot live without a weekly neck and shoulders massage—and of course, family home evening. She now calls the Gold Coast home whenever she returns to Australia to visit family.

0 26575 09355 1